KU-768-152

THE BEST WINES IN THE SUPERMARKETS 2015

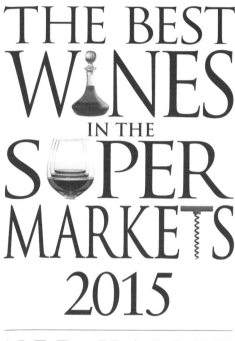

NED HALLEY

foulsham

LONDON • NEW YORK • TORONTO • SYDNEY

W. Foulsham & Co. Ltd
for Foulsham Publishing Ltd
The Old Barrel Store, Drayman's Lane, Marlow, Bucks SL7 2FF

Foulsham books can be found in all good bookshops and direct from
www.foulsham.com

ISBN: 978-0-572-04460-2

Text copyright © 2014 Ned Halley
Series, format and layout design © Foulsham Publishing Ltd

Cover photographs © Thinkstock

A CIP record for this book is available from the British Library

Typeset in the UK by Chris Brewer Origination
Printed and bound in Great Britain by Martins the Printers Ltd

Contents

What's so special about
—supermarket wine?—

The clue is in the title: *The Best Wines in the Supermarkets*. This book is not about all the wines in the supermarkets; it's about the interesting ones.

Let's be honest about this. Most of the wines sold in the supermarkets of Britain are global brands, principally from Australia, South Africa and the United States. They all taste the same. Don't take my word for it. The people who run the biggest supermarket wine departments complain about it louder than anyone else. But they need to do so off the record. They don't want to upset the customers who prefer global brands.

Wise of them. Wine is big business, and the supermarkets have gone a long way towards cornering the market. Eight out of every ten bottles bought for drinking at home comes from one or other of the grocery giants. And while most of it is very ordinary stuff, it makes a nice turn for the retailer. You only have to look at the vast quantity of space devoted to wine displays in the supermarkets to determine how seriously they take this department of business.

Wine makes money. At the everyday level under, say, £6, which still accounts for about 90 per cent of the retail market, the Treasury makes the most. The excise duty on a standard 75cl bottle of still wine is currently £2.05, and to that is added VAT at 20 per cent, lifting the tax take to £2.46 before you get any wine at all. The divvy-up from a bottle for which you pay £6 is £2.46 duty-inc-VAT, 54p VAT on the wine, and £2.95 for the wine itself.

The £2.95, less than half the price, has to be shared between the producer, the shipper and the retailer of the wine. Rest assured, though, the retailer will make the most. Supermarkets are very much more profitable enterprises than winemakers or shippers.

From this rather gloomy calculation emerges an obvious truth. If supermarkets and winemakers want to prosper in this area of commerce, they need to make and sell more expensive wine. This means persuading the market that some wines are worth paying more money for.

It will be a long haul. The supermarkets have been striving for a place in the 'fine wine' sector for decades. Sainsbury's introduced their 'Vintage Selection' range of posh clarets, hocks and other wildly esoteric offerings back in the 1980s, and every one of their rivals has been playing catch-up ever since.

High-value wines remain a chronically exiguous outpost of supermarket retailing. But there is a middle road. Supermarkets now hire the most highly qualified professionals to source their wines. They seek out quality products rather than prestige names, looking in particular for wines they can have bottled under the name not of the maker, but of the retailer. Asda Extra Special, Morrisons Signature, Sainsbury's Taste the Difference, Tesco Finest – you know the sort of thing.

These mid-market ranges now constitute the core of what is interesting on supermarket shelves. They are made under the very noses of the in-house wine teams; they are priced realistically at a level the retailer can profit from (whether or not the same contingency applies to the producer), and because they bear the supermarket's own name, they carry that brand's reputation with them.

In short, the retailers take these wines very much to heart. Nevertheless, most of the supermarkets, most of the time, seem to have large numbers of wines from their own ranges on price promotion. I like to think that they're covering the cost themselves rather than screwing it out of the producers. But I'm probably kidding myself.

As supermarket customers, should we care? I believe we must just leave it to the winemakers of the world to cope with the rapacious practices of UK retailers as best they can. We need to conserve our judgment for the task of working out which of the wines we like, and can afford.

This is the point of *The Best Wines in the Supermarkets*. I taste thousands of the wines they sell, and pick out those I believe qualify under the heading. The sole complication is price. The 500-plus wines I recommend are not simply the most delicious of those I've tried, they are the 500-plus I have liked most at their respective prices. My disposition, perhaps due to an instinctive frugality (I was born in Dundee) tends to see £10 or so as a natural frontier for quotidian purchases and £20 for special occasions. These criteria are loosely reflected in the book.

The premise is that if you shop for wine in a supermarket, you do mind about the price. If you didn't care, or had reasons simply not to deal with a supermarket, you would buy all your supplies from a proper wine merchant. Or, in fairness, if you were even just a little fussy you would examine alternatives such as the Wine Society, a wonderful non-profit organisation founded in 1874 that sells only to its members. It's not all that exclusive, actually. Anyone can join – you don't need to know a proposer – and it has more than 100,000 active members. I would include the Wine Society in this book, but there is no way I can twist its nature or form into anything that could arguably be said to resemble a supermarket.

Back to the point. Price counts in this book, just as price counts in the supermarkets. I give a price for every wine described, but must ask readers to view each one as merely a guide, thanks to the price promotions that are now a perpetual feature of mass grocery retail.

Any supermarket executive will admit – strictly off the record, of course – that the wines that sell best are the ones on promotion. It has became an everyday reality, heightened by the arrival of the two foreign 'discounters', Aldi and Lidl, whose stores always seem to me to be relative havens of promo peace compared to their giant rivals because they choose to incorporate their discounts rather than to fling them into the faces of customers on vast, multi-coloured signs and continual sound-system announcements.

Maybe the current price war will settle down, but for the moment, discount is king, and that goes for wine as much as any other line. Yes, plenty of the deals are phoney. The retailer ups the price for a legally correct period in order to slash it back to the actual price at an illusory reduction. But on own-label wines, this practice is less likely. What chance does one of your own products have if you are obliged to introduce it at an inflated price and return to it at regular intervals?

That's another good reason to avoid yo-yo-price big brands and stick to in-house products.

The promotions to really look out for are the blanket ones. All the major supermarkets do them. It's usually 25 per cent off any wine if you buy six bottles, any mix, at a time. As often as not, wines already on individual discounts are included. Sainsbury's and Tesco do this several times a year – very often in obvious reactive last-minute moves. Marks & Spencer does it online (25 per cent off if you buy any two six-bottle cases) on what is beginning to look to me like a permanent basis. Waitrose does it online on an occasional basis. But everyone sells wine on promotion all the time.

It does all rather skew my scoring system for this book. But look at it this way: if a wine I have scored 9 falls into your hands at £5 instead of the £8 I have quoted it at, you have every chance of liking it even more.

Please take my scoring in the spirit in which it is intended, namely, a subjective indication of how much I liked the wine when tasting it, with the price borne in mind. I write down the scores from my 0 to 10 scale at the moment of tasting, and all those at 6 or above go into the longlist. Few 6- or even 7-scoring wines make the cut, because there is a lot of good wine out there, and I can afford to be sniffy.

Lower-scoring wines that do make it in might be those I've liked but thought overpriced (watch out for them on discount), or feel need more time in bottle, or have looked more alluring on paper than in the mouth. Wines that score 8 are those I've liked a lot. They are recommendable at the prices I have given. A score of 9 signals special merit and value, and the maximum goes to wines I believe deserve nothing less.

In describing the wines, I sometimes make a note of the level of alcohol by volume (abv). This is the percentage of the liquid in the bottle that could be separated from the whole as ethanol, another word for alcohol. Too much of this is bad for health and welfare, and legislators are anxious we should know how much any alcoholic drink includes. For this reason I highlight wines lower than 12 per cent abv and those 14 per cent abv upwards. I hope this is of some help.

Almost all the wines in this book are made entirely or substantially from the harvest of the year stated on the label. If no date appears, the wine will be a blend from the harvests of two or more years. This is routine for some cheaper wines, and need not signify, except for dry whites, which as a rule are the better for being young and fresh.

Finally, a plea to readers to bear in mind that my descriptions and evaluations of all wines are thoroughly subjective and based entirely on my own judgment. I am very well aware that taste is incalculably variable, and that in the case of wine it is especially so. But who would have it otherwise? Here's to wine!

—— *A sense of place* ——

This book categorises the wines by nation of origin. It is largely to follow the manner in which retailers arrange their wines, but also because it is the country or region of origin that still most distinguishes one style of wine from another. True, wines are now commonly labelled most prominently with their constituent grape variety, but to classify all the world's wines into the small number of principal grape varieties would make for categories of an unwieldy size.

Chardonnay, Sauvignon Blanc and Pinot Grigio are overwhelmingly dominant among whites, and four grapes – Cabernet Sauvignon, Grenache, Merlot and Syrah (also called Shiraz) – account for a high proportion of red wines made worldwide.

But each area of production still – in spite of creeping globalisation – puts its own mark on its wines. Chardonnays from France remain (for the moment at least) quite distinct from those of Australia. Cabernet Sauvignon grown in a cool climate such as that of Bordeaux is a very different wine from Cabernet cultivated in the cauldron of the Barossa.

Of course there are 'styles' that winemakers worldwide seek to follow. Yellow, oaky Chardonnays of the type pioneered in South Australia are now made in South Africa, too – and in new, high-tech wineries in New Zealand and Chile, Spain and Italy. But the variety is still wide. Even though the 'upfront' high-alcohol wines of the New World have grabbed so much of the market, France continues to make the elegant wines it has always made in its classic regions. Germany still produces racy, delicate Rieslings, and the distinctive zones of Italy, Portugal and Spain make ever more characterful wines from indigenous grapes, as opposed to imported global varieties.

Among less expensive wines, the theme is, admittedly, very much a varietal one. The main selling point for most 'everyday' wines is the grape of origin rather than the country of origin. It makes sense, because the characteristics of various grape varieties do a great deal to identify taste. A bottle of white wine labelled 'Chardonnay' can reasonably be counted on to deliver that distinctive peachy or pineappley smell and soft, unctuous apple flavours. A Sauvignon Blanc should evoke gooseberries, green fruit and grassy freshness. And so on.

For all the domination of Chardonnay and Cabernet, there are plenty of other grape varieties making their presence felt. Argentina, for example, has revived the fortunes of several French and Italian varieties that had become near-extinct at home. And the grape that (in my view) can make the most exciting of white wines, the Riesling, is now doing great things in the southern hemisphere as well as at home in Germany.

Among the current market trends, the rise of rosé continues apace. Now accounting for one out of every eight bottles of still wine sold, the choice of pink brands has simply exploded. I have certainly found a greater number of interesting pinks than might have been imagined a few years ago, but there are still plenty of dull ones with suspiciously high levels of residual sugar, so choose carefully.

Rosé wines are supposed to be made from black-skinned grapes. After the crush, the skins are left in contact with the juice for long enough to impart a pleasing colour, and maybe some flavour with it, and the liquids and solids are then separated before the winemaking process continues as it would for white wine.

Some rosés are made merely by blending red and white wines together. Oddly enough, this is how all (bar one or two) pink champagnes are made, as permitted under the local appellation rules. But under prevailing regulations in Europe, the practice is otherwise forbidden. Elsewhere in the world, where winemaking is very much less strictly standardised, blending is no doubt common enough.

It is, I know, a perpetual source of anguish to winemakers in tightly regulated European nations that they have to compete in important markets like Britain with producers in Australia, the Americas and South Africa who can make and label their wines just as they please. Vineyard irrigation, the use of oak chips, and the blending in of wines from other continents are all permitted in the New World and eschewed in the Old.

But would we have it any other way? No winemaker I have met in Bordeaux or Barolo, Bernkastel or Rias Baixas seriously wants to abandon the methods and conventions that make their products unique – even with an eye on creating a global brand. And in this present difficult economic climate for wine drinkers (and winemakers) worldwide, this assurance of enduring diversity is a comfort indeed.

Spot the grape variety

The character of most wines is defined largely by the grape variety, and it is a source of innocent pleasure to be able to identify which variety it is without peeking at the label. Here are some of the characteristics to look for in wines from the most widely planted varieties.

White

Chardonnay: Colour from pale to straw gold. Aroma can evoke peach, pineapple, sweet apple. Flavours of sweet apple, with creaminess or toffee from oak contact.

Fiano: Italian variety said to have been cultivated from ancient Roman times in the Campania region of southern Italy. Now widely planted on the mainland and in Sicily, it makes dry but soft wines of colours ranging from pale to pure gold with aromas of honey, orchard fruit, almonds and candied apricot. Well-made examples have beautifully balanced nutty-fresh flavours. Fiano is becoming fashionable.

Pinot Grigio: In its home territory of north-east Italy, it makes wines of pale colour, and pale flavour too. What makes the wine so popular might well be its natural low acidity. Better wines are more aromatic, even smoky, and pleasingly weighty in the manner of the Pinot Gris made in Alsace – now being convincingly imitated in both Argentina and New Zealand.

Riesling: In German wines, pale colour, sharp-apple aroma, racy fruit whether dry or sweet. Faint spritz common in young wines. Petrolly hint in older wines. Australian and New Zealand Rieslings have more colour and weight, and often a minerally, limey twang.

Sauvignon Blanc: In the dry wines, pale colour with suggestions of green. Aromas of asparagus, gooseberries, nettles, seagrass. Green, grassy fruit.

Semillon: Colour can be rich yellow. Aromas of tropical fruit including pineapple and banana. Even in dry wines, hints of honey amid fresh, fruit-salad flavours.

Viognier: Intense pale-gold colour. Aroma evokes apricots, blanched almonds and fruit blossom. Flavours include candied fruits. Finish often low in acidity.

Red

Cabernet Sauvignon: Dense colour, purple in youth. Strong aroma of blackcurrants and cedar wood ('cigar box'). Flavour concentrated, often edged with tannin so it grips the mouth.

Gamay: One of the most distinctive grapes of France, where it is the exclusive variety in the red wines of Beaujolais. Colour can be purple, with a suggestion of blue; nose evokes new-squashed raspberries, and there may be a hint of pear drops, an effect of carbonic maceration, a vinification technique used in Beaujolais. Fruit flavours are notably summery, juicy and refreshing.

Grenache: Best known in the Côtes du Rhône, it tends to make red wines pale in colour but forceful in flavour with a wild, hedgerow-fruit style and hints of pepper.

Malbec: Originally a Bordeaux variety, Malbec has become principally renowned in Argentina, where it thrives in the high-altitude vineyards of Mendoza. Wines are characterised by very dark, dense colour, and by aromas that perhaps fancifully evoke leather and liquorice as well as dark fruits. Flavours include black fruits with chocolate and spice; the wines are often grippy with retained tannin.

Merlot: Dark, rich colour. Aroma of sweet black cherry. Plummy, rich, mellow fruit can be akin to Cabernet but with less tannin. May be hints of bitter chocolate.

Pinot Noir: Colour distinctly pale, browning with age. Aromas of strawberry and raspberry. Light-bodied wine with soft-fruit flavours but dry, clean finish.

Sangiovese: The grape of Chianti and now of several other Italian regions, too. Colour is fine ruby, and may be relatively light; a plummy or even pruny smell is typical, and flavours can evoke blackcurrant, raspberry and nectarine. Tannin lingers, so the wine will have a dry, nutskin-like finish.

Shiraz or Syrah: Intense, near-black colour. Aroma of ripe fruit, sometimes spicy. Robust, rich flavours, commonly with high alcohol, but with soft tannins. The Shiraz of Australia is typically much more substantial than the Syrah of the south of France.

Tempranillo: Colour can be pale, as in Rioja. Blackcurrant aroma, often accompanied by vanilla from oak ageing. Tobacco, even leather, evoked in flavours.

There is more about all these varieties, and many others, in 'What wine words mean' starting on page 150.

Looking for a branded wine?

While the supermarkets' own-label wines – the likes of the Sainsbury's Taste the Difference and the Tesco Finest ranges – are obviously exclusive to the respective chains, branded wines are very often stocked by any number of different retailers.

If you're looking for a favourite brand, do check the index to this book on page 189. If I have tasted the wine and given it a mention, it is most likely to appear under the heading of the supermarket that hosted the tasting. But you might be accustomed to seeing this particular wine in another chain altogether.

I cannot give space in a pocket-sized book to repetitions of notes on popular brands that might very well be sold by each of the supermarket chains. But I do try to keep tasting the bestselling brands in hope of finding something positive to say about them.

Pick of the year: ——*Value wins prizes*——

As I mentioned in introducing this new edition, price plays a part in my scoring system. If money counted for nothing, most of the top-rated wines in this book would cost a lot.

I'm the same as just about everybody else. I like classed-growth claret from good vintages (Tesco has a large selection) and lavish, buttery, over-the-top white burgundies of the kind Waitrose stocks in prodigious quantities. Esoteric Italian reds from Piedmont and Tuscany appeal, and so do regal Spanish vintages from Priorat and the Ribera del Duero; Majestic and Waitrose (again) do a lot of these. But they cost. I do get to taste these wines, and you will find reference to a modest number of them in the pages that follow.

My task in this book is to steer supermarket shoppers in the direction of value-for-money wines. They are what we expect to find in supermarkets. Most of us, anyway. So I have rated the 500-or-so wines recommended here accordingly.

Of the mere 29 that have scored 10 out of 10, just two are priced above £20. They are both champagnes. With value so much in mind, 21 of my top picks are priced at a tenner or under, and two of those came in below the vanishing threshold of £5.

It doesn't signify beyond a parlour-game distraction, but of the top scores, 9 come from France followed by

Spain on 6, New Zealand 5, Australia 4, Argentina and Italy both on 2 and Portugal 1. The retailer chart comes out with Tesco on 6, Sainsbury's 5, Aldi and Waitrose both 4, Asda and Morrisons both 3, the Co-op 2, and Majestic and M&S on 1 apiece. I can confidently assert that these figures give no useful guide to the relative merits of the suppliers concerned.

Red wines

Wine Selection Chianti 2012	Asda	£4.88
Waitrose Mellow and Fruity Spanish Red 2013	Waitrose	£4.99
The Exquisite Collection New Zealand Pinot Noir 2011	Aldi	£6.99
Finest Côtes Catalanes Grenache 2013	Tesco	£7.49
Waikato River Pinot Noir 2012	Morrisons	£7.99
Sister's Run Barossa Cabernet Sauvignon 2011	Tesco	£8.00
The Co-operative Fairtrade Malbec 2012	Co-op	£8.49
DB Family Reserve Petite Sirah 2011	Sainsbury's	£8.50
Comahue Patagonian Pinot Noir 2013	M & S	£9.99
Côtes du Rhône Léon Perdigal 2013	Majestic	£9.99
Pablo the Cubist Old Vine Garnacha 2012	Waitrose	£9.99
Château la Tulipe de la Garde 2011	Sainsbury's	£10.00

Cave de Roquebrun Col de la Serre St Chinian 2012	Waitrose	£10.99
Finest Viña Mara Rioja Gran Reserva 2007	Tesco	£11.49
D'Arenberg The Galvo Garage Cabernet Sauvignon 2008	Asda	£14.47

White wines

Freeman's Bay New Zealand Sauvignon Blanc 2013	Aldi	£5.79
The Exquisite Collection Albariño 2013	Aldi	£5.99
Signature Pedro Ximénez 37.5cl	Morrisons	£5.99
Fossil 2012	Asda	£6.25
Finest Gavi 2013	Tesco	£7.99
Finest Awatere Valley Pinot Grigio 2012	Tesco	£7.99
Taste the Difference Languedoc White 2013	Sainsbury's	£8.00
La Grille Classic Sauvignon Blanc 2013	Waitrose	£8.79
Taste the Difference Riverblock Marlborough Sauvignon Blanc 2013	Sainsbury's	£11.00
Baron de Ley White Rioja Reserva 2008	Morrisons	£12.99

McGuigan The Shortlist Chardonnay 2011	Tesco	£15.00

Sparkling wines

Philippe Michel Crémant du Jura 2011	Aldi	£6.99
Sainsbury's Blanc de Noirs Champagne Brut	Sainsbury's	£22.25
The Co-operative Les Pionniers Vintage Champagne Brut 2004	Co-op	£24.99

Aldi

Until I met Mike James, the wine man at Aldi, I had always blithely assumed that this German-based enterprise bought everything centrally and then distributed it right across the network of the 7,000 stores it operates across Europe and beyond. But no, Mike tells me. All the wines in the 500 UK stores are bought specifically for us, the discriminating Brits. Well, except one, the Toscana Rosso (see under Italian reds), which was the discovery of Mike's counterpart in Austria.

Mike has been in the job for four years. 'I've spent all that time building trust in Aldi wine,' he tells me. Tasting the 50-or-so wines on show at the retailer's event this year, I am left in no doubt of Mike's ability and sincerity.

Aldi might be a no-frills chain – or a 'discounter' in the current rather sniffy phrase – but it wins a lot of prizes for its products, more than 40 per cent of which are sourced in the UK, and is earning a growing loyalty here. The wines, obviously enough, come from producers abroad, but they include many genuine value buys. I noticed that every single one of the still wines put up for tasting came in a screwcap bottle, and I have to say that the prices are really no lower than many of the offerings from the giant supermarkets. But the quality is consistent and some of the wines are inspired. And that counts for a lot.

RED WINES

AUSTRALIA

8 **Bushland Estate Shiraz 2013** £4.99
Much-improved brand has warmly ripe, gently spicy blackberry fruit and a briskly clean edge; 14% alcohol.

CHILE

7 **Andara Merlot 2013** £3.99
Little bit of dark chocolate at the centre of this cherry red, finishing neatly dry.

8 **Estevez Cabernet Sauvignon Carmenère 2012** £4.99
Deep colour and correspondingly intense black fruit is healthily ripe, spicy and balanced; for carnivores.

7 **Estevez Carmenère 2013** £4.99
I like to think the rich colour of this wine is carmine (it's why the grape is so named) and it is indeed a distinctive blackly ripe and satisfying style, perhaps lacking the backbone of the blend immediately above.

FRANCE

7 **Vignobles Rousselet Malbec 2013** £4.49
Grippy but fleeting southern Vin de France has some brambly charm.

8 **Venturer Costières de Nîmes 2012** £4.99
Spicy ripe Midi wine has substance rather than weight and the roasted tension in the fruit of sun-baked grape skins. Good winter red.

9 **The Exquisite Collection Anjou Rouge** £5.99
Non-vintage pure Cabernet Franc from the Loire tastes a lot like a nifty Chinon with ripe redcurrant fruit wrapped in leafy freshness; defined, distinctive flavours.

RED WINES

FRANCE

7 **The Exquisite Collection Fleurie 2013**   **£6.49**
In effect, a decent Beaujolais Villages with likeably typical squishy raspberry fruit.

ITALY

8 **Toscana Rosso**   **£4.29**
From two parts Sangiovese, the Chianti grape, and one of Cabernet with Merlot, a light-coloured but well-formed black-fruit blend with clean Italian finish; very cheap.

8 **Venturer Nero D'Avola 2013**   **£4.99**
Convincing density of colour and roasted fruit in this Sicilian pizza red, after you get over the boiled-sweet nose and whiff of brimstone.

N. ZEALAND

10 **The Exquisite Collection New Zealand Pinot Noir 2011**   **£6.99**
Completely authentic Kiwi red with pale garnet colour, lush raspberry nose and edgy but plumply ripe fruit. I can't fault it, and at the price it's an ideal introduction to this exciting wine style.

S. AFRICA

8 **Cambalala Pinotage Shiraz**   **£3.99**
Typically tarry and savoury midweight red, mainly from the Cape's indigenous black grape, is a proper bargain.

SPAIN

7 **Budavar Merlot Cabernet**   **£3.49**
Homely midweight party red's name suggests Bulgarian origin, but it's from La Mancha. At this price, it tastes good.

8 **Toro Loco Reserva 2010**   **£4.99**
Wholesome blackcurrant aroma and attractive garnet colour in this oaked Utiel-Requena wine benefiting from years. Mostly Tempranillo and Garnacha (the Rioja grapes).

RED WINES

SPAIN

🍷 **7** **Venturer Old Vines Garnacha 2013** £4.99
From Cariñena, a macerated light red in the Beaujolais
style to drink cool in summer.

🍷 **8** **Baron Amarillo Rioja Reserva 2009** £6.29
Colour's going a dignified orange to match the pretty
label; a fading wine with lingering charm.

PINK WINES

ARGENTINA

🍷 **8** **The Exquisite Collection Mendoza Rosé**
2013 £5.99
Strawberry-scented Malbec with big colour and brisk
fruit, finishing crisp and dry; not cheap by Aldi's
standards, oddly.

FRANCE

🍷 **8** **The Exquisite Collection Côtes de Provence**
Rosé 2013 £5.99
Attractive vin gris colour, fresh, floral dry style in the
elegant Provençal tradition.

SPAIN

🍷 **9** **Grapevine Tempranillo Garnacha Rosé**
2013 £3.29
Splendidly lurid magenta colour, slightly sweet
pomegranate fruitiness and a healthy freshness all cohere
into the bargain rosé of the day.

WHITE WINES

AUSTRALIA

🍷 8 **The Exquisite Collection Limestone Coast Chardonnay 2013** £5.99
Unoaked but sleek, even creamy, Aussie standard fare delivers fruit, balance and value.

🍷 8 **The Exquisite Collection Clare Valley Riesling 2013** £6.99
Familiar limey style to a big-flavoured dry wine made to match Asian dishes.

🍷 8 **Vignobles Rousselet Sauvignon Blanc 2013** £4.49
Crisply green grassy Vin de France is geographically rootless but convincingly flavoursome.

🍷 9 **Chenin Blanc IGP** £4.99
The GP (Géographique Protegée) is the Loire Valley, and the wine a deliciously dry, crisp and lively white to match poultry or fish; anonymous but remarkable.

🍷 8 **Chardonnay IGP** £4.99
Mediterranean generic has ripe-apple fruit and a working balance between Chardonnay sweetness and citrus acidity; you get what you pay for.

🍷 9 **The Exquisite Collection Bordeaux Sauvignon Blanc 2013** £5.29
Elegant sunny-ripe and lushly fresh classic Bordeaux Sauvignon at a giveaway price; as good as several of the big-name brands I've tried from the 2013 vintage.

🍷 9 **The Exquisite Collection Touraine Sauvignon Blanc 2013** £5.29
Nice prickle in this Loire seagrass-fresh and long green-fruit-flavoured classy Sauvignon that you could pass off as Sancerre.

FRANCE

WHITE WINES

8 The Exquisite Collection Muscadet Sèvre
et Maine Sur Lie 2013   £5.99
Edgy but not eye-watering crisp Loire mussel-matcher
is not particularly cheap, but it's the real thing; 11.5%
alcohol.

7 The Exquisite Collection Picpoul de Pinet
2013   £5.99
Fashionable Mediterranean oyster-matcher has a shade
of the trademark piquancy, but could do with a drop of
lemon.

8 The Exquisite Collection Sud de France
Sauvignon Blanc Viognier 2013   £5.99
Bizarre grape blend works unexpectedly well; an
aromatic, plump, ripe but perfectly dry refresher with a
twang.

7 Alsace Pinot Blanc 2013   £6.99
Rare bird tastes as it ought, of green-tinged white fruits;
could be crisper.

7 Pinot Grigio Delle Venezie   £4.39
Little bit of smoke on this non-vintage dry wine but the
main draw is the price; 11.5% alcohol.

7 Venturer Vermentino 2013   £4.99
Sherbet nose, spring-blossom white fruit, delicate and
gentle dry aperitif wine from Sicily.

8 The Exquisite Collection Gavi 2013   £5.29
Very decent example of this mildly exotic Piedmontese
dry white from Cortese grapes; fresh white-orchard fruit
with a gentle citrus twang.

WHITE WINES

10 Freeman's Bay New Zealand Sauvignon
Blanc 2013 £5.79

Look at the price! It's like some sort of loss-leader for the entire Kiwi Sauvignon industry, an absolutely correct briny-nosed, grassy-nettly-asparagus photofit model of one of the world's most admirable wine styles.

7 Venturer Vinho Verde 2013 £4.99

Softened style of the revived Minho Valley favourite still delivers a bit of green-fruit eagerness; 11% alcohol.

7 Venturer Rueda Verdejo 2013 £4.99

Tropical tastes come through the fruit-salad nature of this easy dry white; could be crisper, but likeable.

10 The Exquisite Collection Albariño 2013 £5.99

Trace of gold colour and tropical fruit in a blockbuster rich-green, crisp and satisfying dry white from Rias Baixas with a lemon-tang lift at the finish; very, very good at this price.

SPARKLING WINES

8 Crémant de Loire £6.99

There's a giveaway caramel note on the nose of this Chenin-Blanc-based frother, giving way to a brut-style (keenly dry) fresh fruitiness. You don't get much of this in the UK and it makes a pleasant discovery.

10 Philippe Michel Crémant du Jura 2011 £6.99

They've updated the bottle (very smart), but this is still Aldi's foundation flagship fizz – and fantastic value. A single-vintage sparkler from east of Burgundy and all from Chardonnay, it has eager ripe-apple fruit, healthy mousse, crisp brut style and a refreshing vigour.

9 Champagne Veuve Monsigny Brut £12.99

So much of the champagne game is made up of imagery that comparisons can be invidious, but this is surely excellent by any measure. Nice brioche pong, busy tiny-bubble sparkle, lush, creamy but correctly crisp flavour; champagne all the way at a deeply unchampagne-like price.

8 Prosecco Superiore Valdobbiadene £7.29

I've tasted this under other labels and it's good; very pale, vigorous mousse, pear and elderflower nose, plenty of white orchard fruit and perfectly dry; 11% alcohol.

8 Contevedo Cava Brut £4.89

Pale, typical Catalan frothy dry fizz at a very low price indeed; 11.5% alcohol.

Asda

As far as wine goes, Asda is on equal terms, at the very least, with its rivals among the Big Four supermarkets.

That's my judgment on the basis of tasting a wide selection of new names, new vintages and old favourites from the range this year, not long after going through the same gruelling ordeals at Morrisons, Sainsbury's and Tesco.

As a shopper in Asda, however, you might not readily agree with my conclusion. Finding particular wines and understanding the prices can be a considerable challenge even in the best-stocked Asda superstores, in my experience. In search of several much-liked bottles in one giant branch, I came away with fewer than half the number on my list.

With this proviso in mind, I have plenty of genuinely interesting and good-value wines to recommend here. Good luck finding them. Highlights of the range include keenly priced reds from Australia and both reds and whites from New Zealand. Among Italian whites the Gavi is one of my wines of the year, and the quality runs impressively deep among the red wines from Spain.

Where I have added the words Wine Shop to the wines picked out here, it means the wine in question will only be available from Asda's recently launched dedicated online service. Yes, it really is called the Wine Shop.

The website is clearly set out and simple to operate. You get a choice of about 500 wines. Most of them are also stocked in the stores, but 100 or so are exclusive to the online service, including my brand-name wine of the year, a marvellous dry white from Lisbon. It's called Fossil.

RED WINES

8 **Wine Selection Langhorne Creek
Cabernet Sauvignon 2012** £4.98
Healthy blackcurranty ripe (but not over-ripe) Adelaide barbecue red with 14% alcohol.

8 **Zilzie Merlot 2012** £5.00
Full, round, wholesome, balanced and cheap, this is a rare Aussie 'entry-level' red indeed; 14% alcohol.

9 **Extra Special Yarra Valley Pinot Noir 2012** £7.98
By leading Yarra winery De Bortoli (always a name to look out for) a broad-flavoured earthy summer-fruit Pinot of generously lush style, artfully enriched with creamy oak contact. Good value.

8 **Nepenthe Altitude Pinot Noir 2012** £9.00
Bottle bears four medal stickers, but I refused to be deterred from trying this full-bodied, even robust, Adelaide Pinot, which delivers plenty of strawberries-and-cream (some new oak) ripe juiciness; 14% alcohol.

10 **D'Arenberg The Galvo Garage
Cabernet Sauvignon 2008** £14.47
From a brilliant McLaren Vale producer with a propensity for perplexing names, an attention-grabbing, gently decaying Bordeaux-style (mostly Cabernet) cassis-coffee-cigar-box de luxe wine with added Aussie ripeness and verve, and 14.5% alcohol. Quite brilliant. Wine Shop.

8 **Marques de Casa Concha
Cabernet Sauvignon 2011** £11.98
From a range of upmarket varietals by Chilean giant Concha y Toro, a classic sweetly ripe, beguilingly pure and reassuringly balanced Sunday-roast partner; 14.5% alcohol. Wine Shop.

RED WINES

CHILE

9 **Valdivieso Single Vineyard Merlot 2010** £12.47
I don't care how unfashionable Merlot is. This is the plummiest, juiciest and most satisfying spin on the brisk black-cherry theme, natural and pure in every way and ideally balanced. Viva Chile! Wine Shop.

8 **Domaine Les Barthes Comte Tolosan Malbec 2011** £6.79
Bold and spicy dark red from Toulouse area has chewy Malbec savour but also bright juiciness; a good charcuterie red. Wine Shop.

8 **Extra Special Bordeaux Supérieur Roc-Montalon 2012** £7.25
Merlot-dominated middleweight claret has lifted juicy fruit and vigour.

FRANCE

8 **Extra Special Cabernet Sauvignon 2013** £7.25
Interesting minty and sleek blackcurrant Pays d'Oc has purity and definition. Holds the attention; 14% alcohol.

8 **Extra Special Shiraz 2012** £7.25
If this was an Australian or even Australian-style wine the name Shiraz would be fine, but this is a Pays d'Oc Syrah and tastes like it: purple-bright, sleek, spicy and lushly nuanced, with 14% alcohol. I've deducted a point for nomenclative annoyance.

9 **Domaine Lavigne Saumur Champigny 2013** £7.48
Keen green-leafy and redcurrant, crisp, bold Cabernet Franc from Loire winery Lacheteau (of Kiwi Cuvée fame) is refreshingly pure in fruit and will repay discreet chilling. Wine Shop.

RED WINES

8 **Château Boissezon-Guiraud St Chinian 2012** £7.97
Peppery but not fierce dark Languedoc showing the distinct pungent savour of the underappreciated St Chinian appellation. Wine Shop.

8 **The Original Malbec 2012** £8.00
It's a Cahors wine, but the name of the Malbec grape, it seems, now carries more weight than this antediluvian appellation. Dark and muscular, it is smooth but unoaked and nicely weighted.

9 **Celliers des Dauphins Vinsobres 2012** £10.50
Posh Côtes du Rhône delivers sweet silkiness and long spiced fruit in sophisticated balance. Vinsobres (nice equivocal name) is one of a select few CdR villages with its own appellation; 14% alcohol.

8 **Extra Special Châteauneuf du Pape 2012** £13.50
Modestly priced by prevailing standards, a nice mélange of juicy-spicy black-fruit flavours in mellow harmony, already drinking well; 14% alcohol.

10 **Wine Selection Chianti 2012** £4.88
Maybe it's just me, but this is the ideal Chianti, bright with cherry-raspberry juiciness, perfectly weighted and slinkily fruity all the way to the textbook nutskin-dry finish. The price is incomprehensibly low.

8 **Extra Special Primitivo 2011** £7.50
Roasty ripe briary Puglian food wine (red meat) has a touch of sunburn and pruny centre; proper winter warmer.

FRANCE

ITALY

RED WINES

ITALY

🍷 **8** **Extra Special Barbera D'Asti 2012** £8.00
Intense but bouncy-juicy recognisable wine with a creamy lick from oak ageing and familiar blueberry notes; 14.5% alcohol.

N. ZEALAND

🍷 **9** **Extra Special Pinot Noir 2011** £8.48
Lush but tightly defined classic Kiwi Pinot by redoubtable Wither Hills winery has been 'left to relax for 14 months in French barriques', and tastes pretty chilled to me; very good price.

PORTUGAL

🍷 **8** **Conde de Vimioso 2011** £8.50
Mystery red is half indigenous grapes, half Cabernet and Syrah, but tastes all Portuguese – pungent with clove and spice amid likeably austere black fruits. Wine Shop.

S. AFRICA

🍷 **8** **Extra Special Fairtrade Pinotage 2013** £7.00
Lightish in weight and density but not lean (and 14% alcohol) with hallmark pungent tarry fruit and lots of spicy savour.

SPAIN

🍷 **8** **Casa Luis Tinto 2012** £4.00
'Luis' house red', I believe this translates as; mostly Tempranillo from Cariñena, it's juicy, ripe and natural, and weirdly cheap.

🍷 **9** **Noster Nobilis Priorat 2010** £6.98
Gamey-sinewy dark toasty-oaked briary Garnacha-Carignan food red from cult wine region is a gift at this price; 14.5% alcohol.

RED WINES

9 **Gran Bajoz Toro 2010**   £8.00
Long-oaked roasty-spicy macho Tempranillo from admirable Toro denomination has well-wrought intensity and warm savour; 14% alcohol.

9 **Extra Special Marques del Norte**
Rioja Reserva 2008   £8.25
Lacy old Rioja is browning at the edge of the colour and showing a genteel gamey decay in the sweet, plump, silky fruit; still finely defined and gripping, though; 14% alcohol.

8 **Bierzo El Pajaro Rojo 2013**   £10.97
Purple, inky, sweetly ripe but grippy and dry-finishing Castilla y Leon food red (roast pork) of distinct and distinctly Spanish style. Wine Shop.

8 **CVNE Imperial Reserva Rioja 2008**   £19.95
Suitably imperious vanilla-rich and gorgeously plump and minty classic still has years of life ahead of it, and 14% alcohol.

SPAIN

WHITE WINES

9 McGuigan Black Label Reserve
Chardonnay 2012 £7.97
Old-fashioned sweet-apple and peachy oaked Chardy has richness and balance and individual character, all at a competitive price. Wine Shop.

8 McGuigan Bin 9000 Semillon 2007 £12.97
It must have been a moment of distraction. Got home to find my note on this was confined to one word: 'Great'. And so it was, even if I cannot elaborate. For lovers of mature Hunter Valley Semillon, strongly recommended; 11% alcohol. Wine Shop.

8 Cono Sur Bicicleta Gewürztraminer 2013 £7.50
Old friend has perfume of lychee and roses, quite sweet matching fruit and an agreeable spiciness, finishing crisp.

8 La Maison Elyse Sauvignon Blanc
Colombard 2013 £4.00
Crisp, tangy-grassy very dry party white has nicely contrived fruit-freshness balance for very little money.

9 Picpoul de Pinet 2013 £5.40
Unusually low price for this fashionable Mediterranean seafood partner, but it's a good one: bright, fresh and perky with crisply pungent fruit.

8 Château Salmonière Muscadet de Sèvre et
Maine Sur Lie 2013 £6.50
Apple-blossom and sea-breeze aromas come off this tangy Atlantic mussel-matcher; zesty and keen without being green or tart, as some can be.

WHITE WINES

**8 Domaine Les Tailhades Saint Jean de
Minervois 2012**   £6.57
Grapy-sweet Mediterranean 'dessert' wine to treat as an
aperitif or mid-morning indulgence; this is a good one,
with 15% alcohol. Wine Shop.

9 Extra Special Pouilly Fumé 2013   £9.00
Made by famed Loire producer Joseph Mellot, a river-
fresh Sauvignon with grassy, pebbly zing and a lot of ripe,
enduring fruit flavour; 14% alcohol. Rare quality at this
sort of price.

8 Oscar Brillant Sancerre 2013   £11.00
Classic Loire Sauvignon lives up to the name with plenty
of bright fruit.

8 Vincent Carême Vouvray Spring Sec 2012 £11.48
Special wine from the Loire is rich with honeyed ripeness
and yet lemony with twangy acidity; a (just) dry wine
amounting to more than the sum of its parts. Wine Shop.

**8 Brocard Premier Cru Vaillons Chablis
2011**   £15.00
Nice rich eggy Chardonnay whiff from this crisp authentic
Chablis by much-lauded Jean-Marc Brocard. Wine Shop.

9 Jean-Yves Devevey Rully Blanc 2009   £16.96
Mature lush Chalonnais of instantly grabbing quality is
long, rich and mineral in all the best possible ways; by
burgundy standards, a very fair price. Wine Shop.

WHITE WINES

GERMANY

8 **Prinz Von Hessen Riesling 2012**   £10.97
Ripe and racy Rheingau QbA has long, appley fruit and
nicely retained sweetness en route to a brisk finish; 11%
alcohol. Wine Shop.

ITALY

9 **Extra Special Gavi 2013**   £8.00
Steely-edged cryptic Piedmont dry food wine has a rush
of bright orchard fruit and a lingering savour; creamy
pasta dishes, fish and fowl.

8 **Piersanti Verdicchio 2013**   £8.00
Fresh to the point of spritzy but with a blanched-almond
richness to the white orchard fruit, this has appeal. A cut
above other Verdicchios I have come across.

NEW ZEALAND

8 **Wine Selection Marlborough Sauvignon Blanc
2013**   £6.00
Gooseberry style, fresh and grassy – and cheap.

9 **Extra Special Marlborough Sauvignon Blanc
2012**   £7.48
I scored this same vintage 9 last year and here it still is,
by no means dulled by time. It's as briskly juicy, beany-
grassy and delightful as before, and cheaper.

8 **Marlborough Sun Sauvignon Blanc 2013**   £9.00
Ignore the silly newsprint label and relish the verve of
this briny and zesty wine, a cut above the current Kiwi
average.

WHITE WINES

9 **Yealands Estate Single Vineyard Pinot Gris 2012** £12.47

Closer in style to the plump Alsace model than to the vacuous Veneto version, here's a fine expression of the PG with smoky-pungent savour and lavish, long vegetal fruit; fresh and fascinating. Wine Shop.

10 **Fossil 2012** £6.25

Simply outstanding one-off dry wine from the Lisbon area is yellow-gold with an alluring oxidative whiff, even a pale-sherry suggestion, and yet fresh and generously endowed with crisp orchard fruit. Madly underpriced, it's the kind of wine you can drink with anything, and with a lot of pleasure; 14% alcohol. Wine Shop.

8 **Bradshaw Pinot Grigio 2013** £6.00

Puzzlingly named but appreciably crisp PG from western Romania.

8 **Signature Albariño 2012** £8.00

From the Atlantic region of Rias Baixas, an ocean-fresh seafood-matcher with intriguing aromas of cabbage, lemon and racy white fruit.

8 **Extra Special Rueda 2013** £8.25

Clean, tangy and fresh pure Verdejo from dependable region.

SPARKLING WINES

9 Extra Special Louis Bernard Premier Cru Champagne Brut £19.75
Eager but grown-up house non-vintage is a great choice; it tastes evolved as well as fresh and lively. A reasonable price, but look out for a discount anyway.

8 Louvel Fontaine Brut Champagne £24.25
Mellowing but fresh, lemony and long in flavour, an immediately likeable unknown (to me) brand that's worth looking out for at a discount (I have seen it at £12); shelf price is unrealistic.

7 Extra Special Louis Bernard Vintage Champagne 2009 £24.95
New vintage of a perennial favourite, but last year it was the 2004, and this is not yet very enjoyable to drink. Forward planners should wait for a big discount and invest for, say, five years hence.

7 Extra Special Prosecco £6.25
Persistent fizz, peary fruit, quite dry, and best of all, cheap; 11.5%.

9 Fillipo Sansovino Extra Dry Prosecco £8.25
For once overcoming my innate prejudice against Prosecco, I must concede I liked this one: crisp, ripely orchardy fruit, vivaciously fresh and foaming and as dry as it claims to be.

——The Co-operative——

 The mood seemed to me quite cheerful at the Co-op's big 2014 wine tasting. Chatting to the wine-buyers, whose enviable job it is to find and maintain the 350-strong range from around the world, I could quite easily have come away with the impression that all is very well indeed at the retail giant.

Sales of wine through the Co-op's 4,000-plus outlets nationwide are up 5.4 per cent this year over last, even though wine consumption overall is in gentle decline.

So had the scandal surrounding the Co-op Bank, boardroom uproar, financial mayhem and tragic side effects such as the forced sale of the Co-op's own ethically run farms (including its newly planted Gloucestershire vineyard) not been just a little unsettling?

Well, yes, obviously. But we're here to taste the wines. Let them speak for themselves. That's fine with me.

In line with other national supermarket chains, the Co-op is expanding its own-label wine range. Four out of ten bottles sold now bear the Co-op's own imprint, ranging from a couple of the best champagnes to be found anywhere to Fairtrade wines, of which the Co-op is Britain's leading retailer, by a mile.

There is dramatic variation in the availability of the wines. Small convenience stores carry tiny ranges, while more upmarket wines, including the cumbersomely named Truly Irresistible own-label range, are to be found only in the bigger outlets. Sadly, the Co-op does not operate an online wine service.

But the best wines are well worth seeking out.

RED WINES

8 **Linda Mora Malbec 2013** £5.99
Loganberries on the nose of this big dark juice bomb give it an unanticipated frivolity; a robust and cheery Latin red to partner chilli dishes.

10 **The Co-operative Fairtrade Malbec 2012** £8.49
Flagship Fairtrade wine is aged in expensive new oak barrels to plump, creamy effect but not at any cost to the vital juicy-ripe and briary dark-chocolate-centred fruit. Made at the La Riojana winery at Tilimuqui in north-west Argentina, which has provided not just fair wages for the workforce, but a hi-tech water supply and a new school. Drink up!

8 **Trapiche Pure Malbec 2013** £8.99
Leather-scented but not tough blackberry smoothie made without oak lives well up to the name in its natural wholesomeness and warm savour; 14% alcohol.

ARGENTINA

8 **Willow Bridge Estate Cabernet Merlot 2012** £9.99
Approachable dark grippy cassis defined-fruit blend feels natural and finishes crisply.

AUSTRALIA

8 **The Co-operative Truly Irresistible**
Casablanca Valley Pinot Noir 2012 £8.99
Hefty oaked Pinot shows a lot of plump raspberry-strawberry fruitiness as well as dark intensity; 14% alcohol.

CHILE

RED WINES

FRANCE

8 **Les Jamelles Reserve Mourvèdre 2012** £7.49
Well-made, unusual sole varietal with Mediterranean sunny ripeness to the dark briar fruit and a twist of garrigue savour.

9 **The Co-operative Truly Irresistible Chinon 2012** £9.99
A particularly full and ripe example of the likeable leafy reds made from Cabernet Franc in the Loire Valley; hedgerow-fruit aromas, crisply juicy fruit and a brisk twang at the finish. It's OK to drink this cool.

8 **Château Sénéjac 2009** £16.99
Prestige Haut-Médoc estate made a good wine in the auspicious 2009 vintage but it is currently a bit closed up; price is fair, but it's an investment for a few years hence.

HUNGARY

9 **Hilltop Premium Merlot-Kekfrankos 2012** £4.49
Wholesome Merlot-dominated blend has bouncy berry fruit in a well-judged balance; instantly likeable, especially at the price.

ITALY

7 **The Co-operative Truly Irresistible Montepulciano 2012** £8.99
Straightforward purple jolly blackberry-raspy spaghetti red will taste even better at a discount.

8 **Casa Planeta Nero d'Avola Syrah 2013** £9.99
Spicy-rich warmly ripe blackberry-plum Sicilian blend from rated Planeta family estate is a good match for meaty pasta dishes.

RED WINES

ITALY

9 Soprasasso Valpolicella Ripasso 2011 £10.99
Sublime weight to this delightfully rich but gently abrasive speciality red with the cherry sweetness of Valpolicella, and added grip and gravitas from concentrated fruit; 14% alcohol.

S. AFRICA

9 Zalze Sangiovese 2012 £6.99
Cape Chianti – it has the generous fruit brightness of the Tuscan original, and a strong suggestion of the Italian-style nutskin-dry finish too. It's extra ripe and smooth besides, with 14% alcohol, and really rather fun.

SPAIN

8 Muriel Rioja Reserva 2009 £9.99
Friendly vanilla-enriched briskly blackcurranty very typical Rioja, drinking nicely now. I have seen it discounted to £6.66, which makes it a steal.

PINK WINES

FRANCE

8 Coeur de Cardeline Provence Rosé 2013 £8.99
Pale but not wan, delicate but emphatically pink-tasting Riviera rosé is authentic and refreshing.

WHITE WINES

ARGENTINA

8 Linda Mora Torrontes 2013 £5.99
Delicately muscatty dry aperitif wine in a style of its own.

8 The Co-operative Fairtrade Pinot Grigio 2013 £6.99
Interesting spin on the universal PG theme has ripeness of white fruit and crispness of style; a worthy competitor in an overcrowded market.

WHITE WINES

 8 Interlude Semillon 2013   £7.99
If you like the tropical-fruit style, here's a lush but cleanly dry mango-banana-pineapple-melon basket of flavours for aperitif drinking.

 8 Indomita Gran Reserva Sauvignon Blanc 2013   £7.49
Fancifully named but convincing nettly-twangy and copiously fruity dry refresher; dare I say Kiwi-inspired for style?

8 Montes Reserva Sauvignon Blanc 2013   £8.79
Stirring stuff starts with a green nettly nose, moving on to gooseberry and asparagus notes in the grassy, fully ripe fruit; a proper lexicon of Sauvignon sensations, and likeable for it.

 8 Les Jamelles Viognier 2013   £6.49
Easy, mellow, just-dry Mediterranean varietal shows trademark apricot and orchard fruit all nicely lifted by the citrus finish; good white-meat or fish match.

9 Château de la Petite Giraudière Muscadet Sur Lie 2013   £7.25
This one hits the spot with a well-judged cutting edge of citrus acidity to brazenly briny Atlantic-shore white fruit with leesy intensity; good one.

8 Henri Clerc Pouilly-Fuissé 2011   £14.99
Token white burgundy (superstores only) turns out a luscious apple-crumble smoothie with proper Mâconnais minerality; this special-occasion wine would go nicely with lobster.

WHITE WINES

FRANCE

9 **Clos Floridene Graves Blanc 2012**   £17.99
Token white Bordeaux, I suppose I must call this (again, superstores only), but it's of more than token interest. From the classic dry-white Bordeaux cépage of Sauvignon-Semillon with a teaspoon of Muscadelle, it's lush and racy with grassy-exotic fruit flavours discreetly enriched by oak contact and elegantly poised as somehow only the Bordelais know how.

ITALY

8 **Casa Planeta Grecanico Chardonnay 2013**   £9.99
Sherbet-lemon aroma and a corresponding briskness in the white stone fruit is balanced with a crafty almond richness to make an intriguing dry food wine; from a serious family estate in Sicily.

NEW ZEALAND

8 **The Co-operative Explorer's Marlborough**
      Sauvignon Blanc 2013   £9.99
Price is escalating for this hardy perennial, but look out for discounts. Nettly nose, green grassy conventional Kiwi style, a steady standby.

9 **Peter Yealands Marlborough**
      Sauvignon Blanc 2013   £9.99
Zesty and lush style from top Kiwi name of the moment is fuller in fruit than might be expected, and all the better for that; exciting stuff.

SPAIN

8 **The Co-operative Truly Irresistible Godello**
      2013   £8.49
I'm resistant to the branding but persuaded by the distinctive cabbage and sweet-pear aroma and flavour balance in this perky varietal from Galicia.

SPARKLING WINES

9 The Co-operative Les Pionniers Champagne
Brut £16.99
Warmly bready whiff from this lovely bargain champagne
is followed up by mature and developed generous fruit;
Les Pionniers translates as 'the Pioneers' – as in the 19th-
century founders of the Co-operative movement.

10 The Co-operative Les Pionniers Vintage
Champagne Brut 2004 £24.99
Ben Cahill, the Co-op's champagne buyer, promises
this will still be on sale in 2015, but wise to stock up
beforehand at Christmas. It is a well-coloured, brioche-
perfumed, mellow-ripe yet citrus-edged ideally balanced
mature vintage wine out of the top drawer, and a bargain.

7 The Co-operative Prosecco £9.99
Very pale, with a sweet pear nose and matching frothy
fruit; 11% alcohol.

8 Adeletto Prosecco £10.49
Likeable water-white balanced crisp orchard fruit frother
has poise and freshness; 11% alcohol.

Lidl

The best wines at Lidl are elusive. Almost all are sold under the 'Wine Cellar' brand introduced in 2013, famously launched with a £20 classed-growth claret, and ranging through a lot of decent classic wines, particularly from France and Italy.

But quantities are limited. New wines are brought in, a dozen or so at a time, three or four times a year, and in no time they are all sold out. That makes a useful report in this book a little problematic.

I have been buying and trying individual wines from Lidl's 'core' range during the run-up to publication and have picked out a small number for inclusion here. There have been some real disappointments.

But I won't dwell on the shortcomings. Lidl is clearly intent on upping its game. A new range of wines from France, many of them decidedly in the premium class, has been introduced for 2014–2015, and a last-minute tasting has allowed a stop-press report here. My special thanks to Max Halley for his notes on these wines, which I hope signal a new era for Lidl.

RED WINES

 Pays d'Oc Cabernet Sauvignon
Ph. Bouchard 2013 £4.99
Purple but dense Mediterranean red has a leafy quality and
a lick of residual sugar; it has its charm just the same.

 Château Gabarey 2010 £5.49
Small-time Bordeaux has big appeal with plummy dark
fruit, spice and ginger and a curiously enticing note of
rubber; fascinating food red at a bargain price.

 Côtes du Rhône Rochegude
Domaine de Gourget 2013 £5.99
Sweet and spicy new wine from a tricky vintage has lots
of vivid red fruit. A youthful charmer to serve discreetly
chilled.

 Fitou Fonsalis Réserve 2011 £5.99
Grippingly savoury and dark food red (hearty meat dishes)
has spice and intensity; from a Languedoc appellation not
seen as much as of old.

 Médoc AOC Champion 2011 £6.99
Gently spicy generic claret is of middling weight and close
to austere in its purity, but it has real heart. It grows on
you.

Château de Panigon 2011 £8.99
A cru bourgeois Médoc with immediately alluring
mouthfeel and velvet richness; it's still quite grippy, and
promises great things for the future. Good price, good
investment.

RED WINES

8 **Château Venus 2011** £8.99
Violets and black fruit on the nose and pure plump fruit
in this proper young claret from the Graves, south of the
city of Bordeaux.

8 **Gigondas 2013** £9.99
Brooding, dark, southern Rhône red is still youthfully
tannic but already food friendly and relishable.

9 **Mercurey Domaine Grangerie 2012** £9.99
Interesting lemon-grass aromatic on this lush Chalonnais
Pinot Noir; it's rich, savoury and hefty, a delicious surprise
at a surprisingly keen price.

8 **Château Haut Chaigneau 2009** £14.99
Grand Lalande-de-Pomerol claret from a famously ripe
vintage has a pleasantly stewed richness with added
tomato savour; hugely ripe at 14.5% alcohol, but
poised.

8 **Château Haut de la Becade 2008** £16.99
Mature but perky-juicy claret from the grand commune
of Pauillac has masses of lush red fruit; a charmer, and
worth the outlay.

8 **Rosso di Montepulciano 2011** £5.99
Generic red from prestige Montepulciano area of Tuscany
has sturdy dark fruit and something of the ritzy-minty
Vino Nobile style.

RED WINES

ITALY

 8 **Valpolicella Superiore Produttori Associati Soave 2011** £5.99

Healthy cherry aroma from this lightweight Verona classic is followed up by corresponding wholesome fruit; it's the real thing, and attractively fresh considering its antiquity.

PINK WINES

FRANCE

 8 **Château Lignan Côtes du Rhône Rosé 2013** £5.49

Pale but interesting southern pink has a hint of farmyard in the soft summer-fruit nose and a fine freshness.

 9 **Coteaux d'Aix en Provence Nuit de Provence Rosé 2013** £5.99

Pale and elegant Provençal pink has leafy freshness, a hint of pear drop and plenty of gently abrading strawberry fruit. Good price.

WHITE WINES

FRANCE

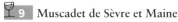 **8** **Bordeaux Blanc Cour de Mandelotte 2013** £5.49

Fresh, simple dry Sauvignon blend is lively and crisp; 11.5% alcohol.

 9 **Muscadet de Sèvre et Maine Domaine de la Vieille Cure 2013** £5.99

Loire bone-dry classic is spot-on, citrussy, stimulating and delicious.

WHITE WINES

8 **Sauternes Château Mauras 2010 50cl** £6.99
Unmistakable pure-gold Sauternes is ambrosially rich and nicely balanced; nice bottle size and nice price.

8 **Mâcon-Villages Domaine des Tourterelle 2011** £7.49
Plump, soft and candied burgundy is forgivably sweet and artfully balanced.

8 **Bourgogne Hautes Côtes de Beaune de Marcilly 2011** £7.99
Buttery popcorn nose but fresh and bright, a likeable Burgundy Chardonnay.

8 **Pouilly-Fumé Les Vignes de St Laurent L'Abbaye 2013** £8.99
Cheery canned-pineapple perfume on this Loire Sauvignon gives way to a contrastingly crisp and flinty classic fruit; good value.

9 **Montagny 1er Cru Les Bouchots 2013** £10.99
Lavish oaked burgundy smells and tastes as plush as it looks in its pardonably over-the-top package; delightfully balanced and extravagant special-occasion wine.

SPARKLING WINES

9 **Champagne Bissinger Brut 37.5cl**   £6.99
Deep and rich with creamy flavours, an extraordinary champagne of truly satisfying depth and length, with lots of Pinot Noir character (my guess); the bargain half-bottle of the year.

9 **Champagne Comte de Senneval Brut**   £12.00
Light style but convincingly vivid and fresh champagne offering terrific value.

9 **Comte de Brismand Champagne Brut**   £12.99
Consistent lemony-fresh and lively non-vintage champagne is easy-drinking, with no sign of greenness, and jolly cheap.

8 **Champagne Comte de Senneval
Premium Brut Rosé**   £16.99
Elegant colour and macerated strawberry on the nose get this ritzy fizz off to a flying start; round and rich, but in fine balance.

Majestic

I've got my eye on Majestic. Changes are afoot.

In the 30-odd years since the chain first came to notice under the ownership of Giles Clarke – now the head honcho of English cricket, curiously enough – it has grown from a handful of warehouse branches in London to a publicly quoted major network with more than 200 outlets nationwide.

While other high street chains have been all-but extinguished, Majestic has sailed – majestically – on. The business has prospered, I believe, from making the wine-shopping experience a pleasant one. The stores are accessible and larky, and staffed by knowledgeable enthusiasts. There's a minimum purchase of six bottles (it used to be 12) so you need a car. But there's always free parking.

Alternatively, you can order from the website (very slick) and get free delivery. But it's a lot more fun to visit the store.

Be prepared. There will be up to a thousand wines on display, a great number of them on offer at promotional prices. Typically, the reduced price will be contingent on the purchase of two bottles. Until this year, the usual discount was 20 per cent. Now, in one of the changes I mentioned earlier, it's 25 per cent.

A sign of the times? Very probably. After decades of continual profits growth, Majestic has lately admitted to a rare downturn in earnings. It's certainly due to the overall shrinking of the market for wine and other drinks, although Majestic, along with other retailers, has at the same time recorded a rise in the sale of 'fine' wines costing £20-plus. Wealthier wine lovers, it seems, have never had it so good.

The widening social gap suggested by this trend seems to be reflected at Majestic. Value wines appear fewer. At this year's tasting of 140-odd wines from Majestic, less than a third were priced at under £10.

But once the prevailing discounts were applied, that figure was nearer to a half. And there's the thing. Majestic is, and always has been, an epic discounter. Once you've understood this, it can be a source of good value. Many of the wines are great, and the overall choice leaves most of the supermarkets in the shade.

The prices I quote for the wines on the following pages are the standard ones. Expect to pay 25 per cent less on the right day.

RED WINES

ARGENTINA

8 **P15 Malbec 2013** £11.99
The cryptic name refers to a road running through the vineyard in Patagonia; the wine is a rugged, roasty outdoor red of healthy charm in the leather-perfumed, spicy Argentine manner.

AUSTRALIA

8 **Wirra Wirra Scrubby Rise 2012** £9.39
Wholesome Shiraz-Cabernet Sauvignon blend has such nifty weight and balance that it's bordering on the elegant in spite of the bucolic name; 14.5% alcohol.

8 **Hamilton Block Cabernet Sauvignon 2012** £12.99
Instantly likeable Coonawarra Cabernet has satisfying juicy savour and natural ripeness. Safe bet.

CHILE

8 **Con Amigos Malbec 2013** £9.99
Familiar Chilean spin on the Malbec: dense but softly yielding black fruit and smooth texture from oak ageing.

FRANCE

8 **Pied Tanqué Rouge 2013** £5.49
Tacky petanque-player label, but a very friendly Mediterranean Merlot-Cinsault red with raspy-but-ripe briar fruit and no particular faults. Rare bargain.

9 **Château Livran 2010 37.5cl** £5.99
A half-bottle of a well-known Médoc cru bourgeois from a fine vintage at this price is a bargain indeed. It's a ripe black-fruit slinky claret already drinking very nicely, and will no doubt develop for years.

RED WINES

10 Côtes du Rhône Léon Perdigal 2013 £9.99
From its dark depths of colour and density it chucks up a lovely minty-heathery-sweet garrigue pong and delivers equally enthralling ripe, savoury, spiky fruit in toothsome balance; just perfect and very attractively packaged, too. Promo price has been as low as £6.66.

8 Lirac Domaine des Garrigues 2012 £9.99
Grippy clinging sweet but pleasingly abrasive hedgerow-fruit southern Rhône red has substance and lipsmacking savour. A style legitimately compared to that of neighbour Châteauneuf-du-Pape.

8 Louis Jadot Beaujolais Lantignié 2012 £11.99
Dense in purply colour and in perky raspberry fruit, this is an unusually tight, crisp kind of Beaujolais, built to last.

8 Nicolas Potel Bourgogne Pinot Noir 2012 £12.99
Pale and pointy with fine definition and good length, this is a smart red burgundy for the contemplative purist.

8 Château Tour du Haut Moulin 2007 £14.99
The colour's still dark and dense, but you sense this Haut-Médoc cru bourgeois will shortly go over the hill; not yet, though – it's a firmly formed blackcurrant and plum mature claret for discriminating fogeys.

8 Crozes-Hermitage Les Saviaux Domaine Michel Poinard 2012 £15.99
Typecast purply violet-scented nose on this lush, pure Syrah, northern Rhône, brimming with spicy-silky blackberry fruit; keep it a few years if you can find the willpower.

RED WINES

8 Cabardès Esprit de Pennautier 2011   £19.99
Blood-red blockbuster from obscure Midi appellation
has a robustly spicy southern style (lots of Syrah) with a
bitter-chocolate centre to the flowing, silky-creamy-cassis
fruit. It grows on you; 14.5% alcohol.

9 Domaine de la Gaffelière St Emilion 1996 £19.99
A generic Merlot-based wine from a 1er Grand Cru
Classé estate, this browning, sweetly milky-coffee-nosed
St Emilion is in wondrous maturity: delicate cassis-cigar-
box aromas and corresponding silky but gripping long
black-fruit flavours.

8 Nicolas Potel Maranges 1er Cru 2012   £19.99
A nice (Côte de) Beaune to chew on, this has plump
strawberry ripeness, creamy texture and crisp finish;
colour is just a shade up from rosé, but don't be deterred.

8 Primitivo Natale Verga 2013   £8.99
Agreeably frazzled black-fruit Puglian red-meat wine has
spicy savour and comforting tannic grip.

8 Pasqua Passimento 2011   £11.99
Indecipherably messy label is a turn-off, but this is a
joyously plump and ripe variation on a Valpolicella
theme, made partly with concentrated grape juice to give
a dense raspiness to the sweet cherry fruit, most of it from
Merlot rather than the usual Corvina; 14% alcohol.

FRANCE

ITALY

RED WINES

ITALY

9 Tommaso Bussola Valpolicella Ripasso Superiore Ca' del Laito 2010 £21.00

Gorgeous, intense, dried-grape-reinforced, chocolate-and-coffee infused, sweetly ripe but bone-dry-finishing contrivance with tangy acidity has huge charm to match the huge price; 14.5% alcohol. Forgive the ghastly label, and try it.

NEW ZEALAND

9 Craggy Range Te Kahu 2011 £19.99

Mostly Merlot plus other Bordeaux varieties, this is something like a pricy, precocious claret, only better. Very dark purple with a bitter-chocolate-coated-cherry pong, it has long, lush, silky and balanced fruit. Sumptuous.

8 Escarpment Pinot Noir 2011 £22.00

On the brink of describing this Martinborough wine as edgy, I pulled back. No, seriously, it's a characteristically dark ripe cherry-raspberry-minty Kiwi Pinot with creamy richness and a good grip.

SOUTH AFRICA

8 The Caracal 2011 £8.99

Bordeaux-grape blend roasty-ripe, toasty-oaked muscular but silky Stellenbosch red-meat wine is 14% alcohol.

8 Parcel Series Shiraz 2012 £8.99

Artfully weighted (but 14.5% alcohol) Western Cape oak-matured barbecue red has long flavour, dark savour and gentle spice.

SPAIN

8 Calima Garnacha Tinto 2013 £7.99

Impactful poster-graphic label draws the eye to this briar-ripe Catalan red with sunny juiciness.

RED WINES

8 El Cometa del Sur Tinto 2013 £7.99

The Comet of the South, as it translates, is quite racy in its abounding spicy blackberry fruit; a clever Catalan contrivance from Syrah, Garnacha and Carignan; 14% alcohol.

9 Ramón Bilbao Single Vineyard Rioja 2012 £9.99

Inky-black young wine has plumpness and juiciness and instant appeal; recognisably Rioja, but made, I believe, without oak.

9 Viña Eguia Rioja Gran Reserva 2004 £13.49

Sweet bright aroma and a real attack of delicious blackcurrant-and-cream classic Rioja fruit in this mature wine from a great vintage; it still has a gentle grip of tannin. Has been discounted down to £8.99, which is a serious bargain.

8 Pesquera Crianza 2011 £25.00

From a famous estate in Ribera del Duero, a darkly savoury and sleek liquorice-mint-prune-cassis muscular red in its youth, creamy with new-oak contact. You do get what you pay for; 14.5% alcohol.

9 Edna Valley Pinot Noir 2012 £12.99

A reminder of the sweet-but-balanced joys of Californian Pinot, this is gloriously juicy and refined with intense soft-summer-fruit ripeness that somehow chimes with nature; 14.5% alcohol.

PINK WINES

 7 **Pied Tanqué Rosé 2013** £5.49
Vanishingly pale dry Mediterranean party pink is dry,
fresh and cheap; 11% alcohol.

 8 **Château de Pigoudet La Chapelle Rosé
2013** £10.99
The light smoked-salmon colour and strawberry nose on
this Coteaux d'Aix-en-Provence deliver crisp pink fruit in
the authentic fresh and edgy style.

 8 **Miraval Rosé 2013** £17.99
Flagon-shaped bottle shows off the coral-salmon colour
of this agreeable, even elegant, Provence dry wine to good
effect. Its principal appeal is, I suppose, that it comes from
the vineyard of film stars Brad Pitt and Angelina Jolie.

 8 **Château de Berne Rosé Côtes de Provence
2013 1.5l** £27.50
Spectacular squared magnum looks like a giant perfume
bottle and shows off the pale salmon colour to a T.
Wholesome pomegranate nose, fresh soft-summer-fruit
style, dry, brisk and fresh. Fun party piece.

WHITE WINES

8 **Santa Ana Sauvignon Blanc 2013** £8.99
Layered flavours of gooseberry and asparagus with briny seasoning make this a fascinator; assertive, attractive wine.

9 **Catena Barrel-Fermented Chardonnay 2012** £12.99
Perennial treat from the maestro of Mendoza is creamy-lush and yet wildly fresh; world-class oaked Chardonnay.

7 **Santa Rita 120 Viognier 2013** £8.99
Old friend, new price, but a likeable crisp'n'dry spin on the superannuated Viognier white with nostalgic hints of apricot and fresh pineapple.

8 **Montes Alpha Chardonnay 2012** £11.75
Extravagant new-oaked Casablanca wine has handsome lemon-gold colour and a lick of butterscotch amid the fine mineral fruit. Shameless indulgence; 14% alcohol.

8 **Lacheteau Réserve Sauvignon Blanc 2013** £7.99
Loire-style Vin de France is nettly-fresh and impressively long in flavour; 11.5% alcohol.

8 **Villemarin Picpoul de Pinet 2013** £8.99
Nicely developed fruit in this fashionable Mediterranean oyster wine, with a tangy twist of lemon acidity.

8 **Château du Cléray Muscadet de Sèvre et Maine Sur Lie 2013** £9.99
The fruit is well ahead of the acidity here, so it's flavoursome as well as bracing in the proper Muscadet manner; pleasing, defined, briny, mussel-matching seaside refresher.

WHITE WINES

8 **Côtes du Rhône Blanc Léon Perdigal 2013** £9.99
Exotic southern peaches-melon standout dry white of
herbaceous lushness and citrus edginess for salad days.

8 **Pierre Sauvion Sauvignon Blanc 2013** £9.99
Val de Loire varietal doesn't look cheap, but it has a
bracing lemon-grass style and a lot of crisp refreshment
to offer; 11.5% alcohol.

8 **Valençay Le Clos du Château 2013** £9.99
It's a long-flavoured grassy-twangy Loire Sauvignon with
an unexpected added measure of Chardonnay; very easy
drinking.

9 **Bernard Fouquet Vouvray Domaine des
Aubuisières 2013** £11.75
Sublime Loire Chenin Blanc has perfect poise between
caramel-honey lush and mineral-pure freshness; a rare
and remarkable aperitif wine.

8 **Reuilly Cuvée Nathalie 2013** £11.99
Beguiling toffee hint on the nose of this lush but stony-
bright Loire Sauvignon of real charm; a natural match for
river-fish dishes, somehow.

8 **Nicolas Potel Bourgogne Chardonnay
2012** £12.99
Well-coloured, toffee-nosed, ripe and lush dry style from
'the heart of Burgundy', by which I assume the posh Côte
d'Or bit is to be inferred; I can believe it.

WHITE WINES

**Mâcon-Villages Les Roches Blanches
Louis Jadot 2013**   £13.49

Big-name burgundy looks the part and tastes it, too.
Top wine from on-form Mâconnais is sweet-apple ripe
and minerally bright, with satisfying weight and length;
Chardonnay with a proper shine.

**Louis Latour Pouilly-Vinzelles En Paradis
2012**   £14.99

As a role model for the white wines of the Mâconnais,
this will do very nicely. You get textbook sherbet-mineral
Chardonnay perfume and a rush of racy but exotic fruits
with notions of green pepper. De luxe burgundy made
without oak, and at a fair price.

**Domaine des Baumard Clos du Papillon
Savennières 2009**   £25.00

Cult Loire Chenin Blanc is so gorgeous it arguably
warrants the price; honeysuckle and a whiff of Muscat
perfume the luscious orchard fruit and you get textbook
Chenin scythe-like acidity to complete the perfect balance.

Custoza Cantina di Custoza 2013   £8.99

Lots of colour and an alluring sweet blanched almond
and blossom nose lead to a soft but fresh and delicate dry
white to match creamy pastas and fish.

Contesa Pecorino 2013   £9.99

Jolly label and alluring scrambled-egg nose make you
want to know more; it's a dry, brisk wine with sweetly
ripe white orchard fruit and a plush linger in the mouth.

WHITE WINES

ITALY

8 **Stella Alpina Pinot Grigio 2013** £11.99
It's from sub-Alpine Alto Adige, crisp, long and mineral, a superior sort of PG at a superior sort of price.

NEW ZEALAND

9 **A Sticky End Noble Sauvignon Blanc 2011 37.5cl** £14.99
Gold-bullion colour to this Marlborough nectar is fully matched by the richness of the honeyed fruit and leitmotif of the citrus balance; it's ambrosial, much in the way of a regal Sauternes, and as such is fair value; 10.5% alcohol.

8 **Waimea Estate Gewürztraminer 2013** £14.99
A lot of Gewürz, even from Alsace, is dull and cloying, but this Kiwi is tightly defined, even crisp and in the proper spicy manner. Good one, at a price.

8 **Saint Clair Pioneer Block Riesling 2013** £17.49
You get a lemon-sherbet tingle and a lot of racy fruit laced with apple sweetness, delicate in an ethereal fruit-juice sort of way. Marlborough moselle Spätlese, just about; 9% alcohol.

SPAIN

8 **El Cometa del Sur Blanco Terra Alta 2013** £7.99
I am well-disposed to anything to do with comets, and very much liked this new one (to me), a white Grenache from Catalonia with apricot pungency and plenty of plump white fruit.

9 **Godello As Caixas Martin Codax 2012** £9.99
Lavish Galician trendy varietal from region's top co-op has a beachful of seagrassy white fruit and buckets of lemon tang. Big wine for authentic Spanish tapas or paella.

WHITE WINES

  **Deusa Nai Albariño Marqués de Cáceres
2013** £13.49
The famed Rioja bodega's name might catch the eye. This
Rias Baixas (Galicia) might be off their patch, but it's on
target – a rich but very tangy rush-of-fruit seaside bracer.

SPARKLING WINES

 Nyetimber Classic Cuvée 2009 £35.99
From the same grape varieties as proper champagne, but
grown in Sussex, a distinctly champagne-like, eagerly
sparkling, biscuity-ripe single-vintage wine of mellow
maturity and long flavour; a marvel. As long as it's
discounted to under £30, good value, too.

 **Crémant de Loire L'Extra par Langlois
Brut** £14.99
Floral fresh frother from Chenin Blanc grapes is bottle-
fermented in the same way as champagne, and full of
lively fruit. Crémant de Loire wines are inexplicably
neglected, and this one is cracking value, sometimes
reduced to £9.99.

J de Telmont Grande Réserve Brut £24.99
Majestic's house champagne continues on good form
with bready aroma, crisp orchard and lemon fruit,
mouth-filling generosity; don't pay more than the usual
discounted price, down to £15.99.

Marks & Spencer

Wine-wise, Marks & Spencer is out on its own. Every bottle bears the M&S imprint, and while plenty are no doubt available elsewhere under different labels, many are unique to this one retailer.

It makes comparisons to the main competition, the supermarkets, look rather pointless. But M&S certainly matches or supersedes all its big rivals for quality, diversity and price at every level. Tasting the new wines this year has been a firm reminder.

Particular strengths include remarkable ranges of reds from Argentina and Italy, some revelatory whites from South Africa, and overall, an admirably broad-minded approach to national sources. I tasted, and liked, new wines from Brazil, Lebanon, Georgia, Turkey, and India.

Prices at M&S are steady. There is nothing under a fiver any more, but still a decent selection under £6.50. The choice widens invitingly en route to the £10 mark, and as always, the 'fine' wine end of the spectrum is imaginative and occasionally quirky.

Store promotions are nothing like as frequent or aggressive as those in the big supermarkets, but online, M&S regularly offers 25 per cent off its six-bottle cases if you buy any two or more. That's a very useful discount indeed.

RED WINES

9 **Caleidoscopio Sangiovese Touriga Nacional Caladoc 2013** £7.99

Unlikely pairing of the Chianti and Port grapes with Languedoc curio Caladoc by Mendoza's Santa Julia winery summons up a jaunty, brambly but robustly ripe and grippy pizza red of rare character; 14% alcohol.

8 **Senetiner Bonarda 2013** £8.99

It has the brambly bounce of a Piedmont Barbera with added dark intensity, and that scores for me.

10 **Comahue Patagonian Pinot Noir 2013** £9.99

It looks and smells very much like a southern Burgundy Pinot, which goes to show how well this reputedly agoraphobic grape can travel. Pure, naturally ripe (14% alcohol) soft-summer-fruit style, lush, creamy and elegant – a wonderful advertisement for Patagonia.

8 **Barossa Shiraz 2012** £9.99

Toasty intense blackberry smoothie with welcome rasp of acidity by St Hallett winery is a fine act of balance; 14% alcohol.

8 **The Islander Kangaroo Island Sangiovese 2012** £12.49

From the grape of Chianti made by flying French winemaker Jacques Lurton off-shore from Adelaide, a juicy but substantial grippy red with focused flavours; intriguing.

ARGENTINA

AUSTRALIA

RED WINES

BRAZIL

8 Intenso Teroldego 2013 £9.99

In fairness, it is an intense variation on a varietal more familiar from the sub-Alpine slopes of Italy; chunky bitter-chocolate-centred redcurrant, darkly savoury red with long fruit.

CHILE

8 Luis Felipe Edwards Chilean Merlot Carmenère 2013 £5.29

Cheap and winning dark-chocolate-covered-plum-style party red; a bargain.

8 Los Almendros Fairtrade Cabernet Carmenère 2011 £7.49

Blackcurrant smoothie for barbecues from well-intentioned Viña Los Robles winery in Curico.

ENGLAND

8 Plumpton Estate Red 2013 £10.99

This isn't just jingoism: a proper raspberry red of bucolic charm from a winemaking college in Sussex, styled a bit like a Loire Cabernet Franc; 10.5% alcohol.

FRANCE

7 Beaujolais 2013 £8.49

Decent, juicy, uncomplicated, typical raspberry Beaujolais seems overpriced.

8 Gold Label Merlot 2013 £8.49

Perky Pays d'Oc picnic red with Mediterranean spice and black-fruit savour.

9 Domaine de Rosette Chinon 2013 £8.99

Darkly redcurrant, leafily fresh and lemon-tinged crunchy Loire Valley Cabernet Franc is quite light in weight but firmly knit in flavour and substance; a cracking food red that will respond to gentle chilling.

RED WINES

8 Latour de France Fort de Triniac 2012   £8.99
Robust Roussillon red has deep purple hue, liquorice-and-prune-centred peppery black fruit and a lipsmacking tannic finish; fine cassoulet or roast-meat match; 14.5% alcohol.

8 Château de Saÿe 2011   £9.99
Dark crimson Merlot from Bordeaux right bank is remarkably ripe, even a little sunburnt, giving it a toasty savour that is not entirely down to the oak-ageing.

8 Mâcon Rouge 2013   £10.49
Juicy summer red from Gamay tastes unlike any Beaujolais rendering of the same grape, but has brisk red-fruit charms of its own.

8 Primo de Conti Côtes de Bergerac 2009   £10.99
Inviting intense cassis nose on a correspondingly dense and clingy Cabernet-Merlot-Malbec mix that finishes very clean; ripe vintage (14% alcohol) ageing gracefully.

9 Mercurey Domaine Levert 2011   £13.99
Lovely Burgundy Pinot Noir from the under-reported Chalonnais has limpid ruby colour, heavenly strawberries-and-cream perfume and poised, silky red fruit.

8 Le Haut-Médoc de Giscours 2009   £22.00
Cigar-box generic claret from grand Margaux estate Château Giscours in a famed vintage is well up to the expectations we're entitled to at this sort of price. Lovely special-occasion slinky wine to drink now.

RED WINES

FRANCE

9 **Chambolle-Musigny Les Caves de
la Colombe 2011** £38.00
Lyrically named burgundy lives entirely up to its promise;
creamily silky red fruit in perfect harmony will evolve for
years: a long-term investment.

INDIA

8 **Jewel of Nasik Tempranillo Shiraz 2013** £6.99
Real red wine, quite liquorous, dark and spicy from a
source you'd surely never guess – east of Bombay! It
might well make a match for something fiery.

ITALY

9 **Popolino Rosso 2012** £5.29
If there is a 2013 vintage I haven't seen it, but this one,
which I buy whenever I can, is still deliciously perky with
juicy redcurrant fruit, plenty of healthy intensity and a
twitch of spice; great pasta bargain red from Sicily.

9 **Beneventano Aglianico 2011** £6.49
Densely coloured and textured spicy-ripe blackberry
Campania red has terrific plum-with-skin-on, sweet-but-
grippy wholesome savour; perfect match for tomato-
based pasta dishes, and top value.

9 **Loretto Sangiovese Rubicone 2013** £6.49
Cherry-scented, briar-ripe, deliciously rasping spaghetti
red from the grape of Chianti made in neighbouring
Emilia Romagna region.

9 **Caruso e Minini Perricone 2012** £7.99
Made in Sicily from the indigenous Perricone grape, a
bumper plummy-spicy red of distinctive style with more
than a hint of sun-baked island herby-scrubby savour,
and 14% alcohol. Strongly recommended with meaty
pasta dishes.

RED WINES

8   **Bardolino Cavalchina di Piona 2013**   £8.99
Pale but not weedy, dry, cherry-fruit balanced example of the famed Verona lightweight will chill well, and suit fish pie as well as the usual antipasti.

8   **Pinot Nero Dolomiti 2013**   £8.99
Sub-Alpine dark and minty Pinot Noir is mineral pure and plumped by oak contact.

9   **Renato Ratti Langhe Nebbiolo 2011**   £13.99
Barolo-style slinky strawberry-nose, black-cherry-fruit oaked luxury wine from an irresistibly named producer of very evident ability; 14% alcohol.

8   **Cascina Morassino Barbaresco 2009**   £30.00
Chestnut brown is coming into the ruby colour, and fruity truffle, gamey aromas are infecting the perfume – a glorious gallimaufry of nuance in this maturing Piedmont classic, still tannic and showing no sign of drying out; 14.5% alcohol.

8   **Château Ksara Clos St Alphonse 2011**   £9.99
Dark and intense savoury blackcurrant gripper from hazard-prone Bekaa Valley is toastily oaked and reassuring.

8   **Seifried Estate Nelson Pinot Noir 2011**   £10.99
Light to look at, but a firmly formed strawberry-ripe and substantial proper Kiwi Pinot with creamy silkiness; nice match for duck.

ITALY

LEBANON

N. ZEALAND

RED WINES

N. ZEALAND

9 Quarter Acre Syrah 2011 £14.99

Rich dark minty-spicy-gamey Cornas-like Hawke's Bay wine is exciting and attention-grabbing. Equal in appeal to northern Rhône Syrah counterparts at even higher prices.

SPAIN

8 Jumilla Las Hermanas 2013 £8.99

Dark and smoky Monastrell-Syrah blend from improving Mediterranean region has characteristic bite and 14.5% alcohol; a natural for flame-grilled food.

8 Idrias Abiego Roble 2012 £9.99

From (mainly) Cabernet Sauvignon and Merlot grown in Somontano, a muscular spicy cassis red of heroic ripeness (14.5% alcohol) aged in new oak to toasty effect; grows on you.

TURKEY

8 Anfora Trio 2012 £7.99

Syrah and Cabernet Sauvignon combine with a mystery indigenous grape, Kalecik Karası, to make this slightly tart but healthily fruity and balanced food red; it scores for more than mere curiosity value.

USA

8 Wave Break Merlot 2013 £7.99

Cheap-looking Californian package lets down this nicely poised Morello Merlot (made with the addition of many other varieties in tiny quantities) with lingering flavours and artful nifty definition.

8 Underwood Pinot Noir 2012 £12.99

Hefty, sunnily ripe Oregon wine of unexpectedly intense colour and fruit; very much Pinot Noir, but not as we usually know it.

PINK WINES

FRANCE

8 **Bordeaux Rosé 2013** £7.99
Coral-coloured, crisp, fresh red fruits, dry and safe, from
dependable Bordeaux outfit Sichel; 11.5% alcohol.

8 **Domaine de la Navarre Côtes de Provence
Rosé 2013** £8.99
Trademark pale coral colour and tightly defined crisply
dry red-berry fruits in this neat Provence al fresco pink.

INDIA

8 **Jewel of Nasik Zinfandel Rosé 2013** £6.99
It wouldn't stand up to a chicken madras, but this well-
coloured wine does have some pink fruit, manageable
residual sugar and a degree of freshness; 11% alcohol.

S. AFRICA

7 **Six Hats Fairtrade Rosé 2013** £7.99
Magenta food pink has sweet summer-soft-fruit
plumpness from Pinotage grapes, but finishes quite dry.

SPAIN

9 **Las Falleras Rosé 2013** £5.29
Salmon-coloured, dry, simple, fresh Utiel-Requena pink
with strawberry juiciness and modest 11.5% alcohol.
Scores for value and lack of pretension.

WHITE WINES

ARGENTINA

8 Caleidoscopio Pinot Grigio Fiano Albariño 2013 £7.99
Catch-all blend from Santa Julia estate happens to work well in a fruit-salad sort of way; fresh and nuanced.

AUSTRALIA

8 6285 Margaret River Chardonnay 2013 £12.99
Apple-fresh but creamy classic Aussie Chardy has modern elegance and balance; a wine made to a standard, not to a price, which is what Australia does best.

CHILE

8 Chilean Chardonnay Viognier 2013 £5.29
This sort of blend makes me sigh a bit, but this one delivers plenty of white fruit and vivacity, and is endearingly cheap.

ENGLAND

8 English White Lily 2013 £9.99
Loire-style dry, stony-fresh aperitif wine from giant Denbies vineyard in Surrey; 11% alcohol.

FRANCE

9 Sauvignon Blanc Vin de Pays du Val de Loire 2013 £7.49
Whiff of asparagus launches this delightful green-tinged, grassy, generic Sauvignon on a long flavour trail of exciting quality; 11.5% alcohol.

8 Gold Label Chardonnay 2013 £8.49
The label design remains resolutely unmodernised and this perennial from Languedoc giant Domaines Virginie stays consistently plump and peachy, with a caramel lick and artful citrus twang.

WHITE WINES

8 **Château de Flaugergues Blanc 2013** £8.99
Herbaceous salad dry white Mediterranean wine has a
proverbial mélange of orchard-and-tropical fruits.

9 **Château Moncontour Vouvray Demi-Sec
2013** £9.99
This is not a sweet wine, but a sunshine-ripe dry one with
a kind of wheaty autumn richness. From a Loire village
famed for its 'moelleux' (marrow-unctuous) Chenin Blanc
whites, a superb aperitif and a match too for poultry and
other delicate flavours; 11% alcohol.

8 **Mâcon-Villages 2013** £9.99
Lively, leesy and lush authentic regional unoaked
Chardonnay.

8 **Saumur Blanc Les Epinats 2011** £9.99
Rare Loire white from Chenin Blanc grapes has rich
colour and a waft of honeysuckle, excitingly balanced in
the fruit by the characteristic lemon thrill of the Chenin.
A fine fish wine, as well as a distinctive aperitif.

9 **Viré-Clessé 2012** £11.99
Plush Mâconnais has sleek apple-pie minty-mineral
typical Chardonnay rush of flavour, enriched with
creamy-toffee oak contact; made by serious Beaune outfit
Albert Bichot.

8 **La Tuilerie Pouilly Fumé 2013** £13.99
River-fresh Sauvignon of nettly-zesty verve and lots of
ripe green fruit from famed waterside appellation of the
Loire.

WHITE WINES

8 Le Clos Sainte Odile Obernai Riesling 2011 £13.99

Inspired Alsace wine made at Cave de Beblenheim by one Patrick Le Bastard is spicy-nosed, grapy, long and full but quite dry and lemon-edged.

9 Puligny-Montrachet 1er Cru Les Folatières 2010 £38.00

I'm always willing to try great white burgundies. This one from rising domaine Chavy-Chouet is long, luscious and lemony with years ahead of it; simply gorgeous if you can afford it.

8 Tbilvino Qvevris 2011 £8.99

Fermented in qvevris (huge clay pots), this gold-coloured, exotic-fruit, mildly pungent rancio aperitif wine has genuine charm.

8 Jewel of Nasik Sauvignon Blanc 2013 £6.99

From nascent vineyards east of Bombay, a recognisable Sauvignon of green freshness and easy acidity.

8 Giardini Veneto Tai Pinot Grigio 2013 £6.99

Eight parts Tocai Friulano grapes to two of PG, a cheerily zesty Veneto dry wine with plenty of white fruit, a hint of smoke and just 9.5% alcohol.

8 Grillo 2013 £6.99

Native grape once used only for sticky Marsala now makes positive dry whites in Sicily, such as this generously orchard-fruity, sunnily disposed and food-friendly charmer.

WHITE WINES

ITALY

🍷 **8** **Pinot Grigio Terre Siciliane 2013** £6.99
Green fruit, citrus twang, dry but not too dry, a pleasant
Sicilian twist on the perpetually popular PG theme.

🍷 **8** **Ascheri Langhe Arneis 2013** £12.99
Dry Piedmont wine from local Arneis grape has a
pineapple perfume, nutty creaminess and tropical-fruit
basket of flavours, all fresh, lively and stimulating; stands
out from the crowd.

N. ZEALAND

🍷 **9** **Kaituna Hills Marlborough Sauvignon
Blanc 2013** £9.99
Distinct asparagus note in the perfume and fruit of this
consistently thrilling nettly-fresh perennial made by
Pernod-Ricard-owned Montana/Brancott giant; real
value here.

PORTUGAL

🍷 **8** **Tapada de Villar Vinho Verde 2013** £7.99
Near-spritzy dry and almost austere 'green wine' of the
Minho Valley is softened at the last by noticeable residual
sugar, presumably for the sweet-toothed export market;
10.5% alcohol.

SOUTH AFRICA

🍷 **8** **Journey's End Honeycomb Chardonnay
2013** £9.99
Herbaceous creamy pure Chardonnay, very much in the
Cape style, with bright minerality.

🍷 **8** **Paul Cluver Ferricrete Riesling 2013** £12.99
Ferricrete is topsoil with lots of iron oxide in it. Perhaps
this is identifiably connected to the sterling character
of this plump, grapy and racy-appley aperitif; 10.5%
alcohol.

WHITE WINES

S. AFRICA

9 **Land of Hope Reserve Chenin Blanc 2012 £15.99**
Gold colour and lavish tropical-tangy textbook Chenin fruit fermented in 'Burgundian French oak barrels', some of them new, makes for an extravagantly rich but nonetheless keenly fresh dry white of quite arresting character.

SPAIN

9 **Toque Virtuoso Sauvignon Blanc 2013** **£6.99**
Valencian variation on the theme is in a lemon-mousse style, nutty ripe and gleefully fresh – a complete departure from Loire or Kiwi Sauvignon, and very appealing indeed.

8 **Marques de Alarcon Blanco 2013** **£7.99**
Castilian blend of Macabeo and Verdejo is in an expansive, crisp, orchard-fruit style with freshness and verve.

USA

8 **Charles Smith The Honourable Riesling
2013** **£11.99**
Dry, limey and long-flavoured Riesling from Washington State in the US north-west owes something to the Alsace style in terms of weight and seriousness; an attention-holding aperitif or white-meat wine.

SPARKLING WINES

ENGLAND

8 **English Sparkling Rosé Brut** **£22.00**
Two years ago I gave this Chapel Down, Kent, fizz a score of 10. This more recent bottling is pinker than its predecessor in both colour and flavour – nice mélange of delicate fruits – but maybe less distinctive as a competitor for champagne.

SPARKLING WINES

8 **Marksman English Sparkling Brut
Blanc de Blancs** £26.00
Pure Chardonnay from Ridgeview in Sussex is convincingly close to the champagne model, which it needs to be at the price.

9 **Champagne Oudinot Brut** £25.00
M&S's house champagne is a finely judged, all-Chardonnay, creamy but apple-fresh Côtes des Blancs wine with evident bottle age.

9 **Champagne De Saint Gall Premier Cru
Brut Tradition** £30.00
A 'premium' champagne from prime vineyards, this M&S perennial is on fine form with long, developed fruit in a rich, complex medium of exuberant sparkle. Not a vintage wine, but a special one, warranting the price.

7 **Prosecco Masottina** £9.99
If you like your Prosecco very dry, you should like this lively elderflower fizz; 11% alcohol.

8 **Franciacorta Due Lari di Gatti** £18.99
New-to-M&S Lombardy fizz is maybe seeking to exploit the Prosecco bubble, but this is much more interesting: a brioche-nosed sweet-apple Chardonnay full of flavour and foaming vigour, and briskly dry.

9 **Villiera Brut Natural 2010** £11.99
Stellenbosch pure Chardonnay is made in the same way as champagne, complete with three years' bottle ageing; with mellow gold colour and a lot of enticing yeasty fruit, it's a convincing 'shampagne' for the money.

Morrisons

The big draw this year at Morrisons is the own-brand wines. There is a fast-growing range of mid-price wines under the heading 'Morrisons Signature', and many additions to the everyday own-label choice besides.

Price is a major factor. Morrisons has this year introduced 30 per cent more wines at under £10, announcing that almost 90 per cent of the entire range is priced below a tenner.

The wines I have tasted over the year bear this out. Of 49 described in the following pages 42 are under £10, including 11 below a fiver. Most of them are own-brands, and they're all good. Some of them are simply marvellous.

Along with its rivals among the Big Four, Morrisons continues to discount large parts of the wine range year-round. There are good deals too online, where the dedicated Wine Cellar website has now been incorporated into the overall grocery service site, Morrisons.com.

RED WINES

Morrisons

ARGENTINA

8 **La Bodega de los Altos Andes Malbec 2013** **£4.99**
Firm, dark and spicy roasty-ripe fruit of easy savour in this attractive bargain package.

8 **La Posta Bonarda 2013** **£9.99**
Bonarda is an escaped Italian grape variety that consistently makes likeable Italian-style red wines in South America. This focused juicy food-matcher (pasta, pizza, natch) with its nutskin-dry finish fits the profile.

AUSTRALIA

8 **Signature Limestone Coast Cabernet Sauvignon 2013** **£8.99**
Sunnily ripe but elegantly poised pure Cabernet of, dare I say it, a Bordeaux-like balance. Very easy drinking with a lamb chop.

9 **Wirra Wirra Church Block Cabernet Shiraz Merlot 2011** **£12.49**
Succulent liquorice centre to the bundle of opulent black-fruit flavours that make up this perpetually delicious McLaren Vale classic blend; 14.5% alcohol. Online only.

CHILE

8 **Signature Carmenère 2013** **£5.99**
Sweet plum and marzipan figure in this distinctive black-fruit Colchagua wine, finishing clean and tight.

8 **Santa Carolina Cellar Selection Shiraz 2013** **£6.99**
Strong purple hue, firm blackberry fruit and mellow texture with firm but discreet tannin.

RED WINES

CHILE

9 **Ventisquero V9 Carmenère 2012** £8.99
Bold savoury summer-pudding Colchagua blend (includes 15% Syrah) has been long-oaked to sleek, rich effect, by no means overwhelming the dark, briary and spicy fruit.

8 **Morrisons Claret** £4.49
'Rich and fruity', says the label on this non-vintage, 60:40 Cabernet-Merlot. 'Cheap and surprisingly wholesome' might be nearer the mark. Actually, I quite liked it.

FRANCE

9 **Morrisons Côtes du Rhône** £4.75
It's the price, really, but I did relish the dark, roasty centre to the gently spicy, comfortably ripe fruit. Although non-vintage, the blend is avowedly based on the good 2012 harvest rather than the patchy 2013.

9 **Signature Reserve Claret** £4.99
Non-vintage 60:40 Cabernet-Merlot by redoubtable Bordeaux merchant-maker Sichel is artfully beguiling, a mature-tasting slinky cassis-plum true claret at a great price.

8 **Signature Beaujolais Villages 2013** £6.49
Pale-looking, but lots of juicy raspberry vigour and freshness from a difficult Beaujolais vintage.

ITALY

8 **Villa Verde Montepulciano D'Abruzzo** £4.25
Brambly, non-vintage, quite sweet but perfectly healthy outdoor red (try chilling it) at an amazingly low price.

8 **Signature Montepulciano D'Abruzzo 2013** £6.99
An unusually vanilla-rich variation on the familiar brambly style of this perky red; works well.

Morrisons

ITALY

8 Signature Sangiovese Superiore 2013 £6.99
Dark and firm briar-cherry fruit in this Emilia-Romagna food red has ripeness and grip.

9 Signature Valpolicella Ripasso 2012 £8.99
Souped-up Verona speciality red has fruitcake intensity and cherry top notes to the plump, satisfying weight of flavour; a unique wine style enjoying a well-deserved vogue.

8 Castiglione Barbaresco 2011 £9.99
From Araldica, it looks a bit delicate but takes a firmly friendly grip on the taste buds with its nutty dry cherry fruit and elusive truffle richness; 14% alcohol.

N. ZEALAND

10 Waikato River Pinot Noir 2012 £7.99
Lovely succulent minty-cherry oaked lush wine by Seifried is bright and assertive in fruit flavours, finishing tautly dry and clean. It really stood out, and the price seems more than reasonable.

PORTUGAL

8 Signature Douro Red 2012 £7.99
Porty-nosed dark pungent-briar fruit has a bitter-chocolate centre and grippy outer edge to the flavour; good one, judiciously oak-matured.

S. AFRICA

8 Morrisons Cabernet Sauvignon 2013 £4.49
Where else would you go but the Cape for Cab Sauv at this price level? It's brightly blackcurrant, healthy and balanced.

RED WINES

SOUTH AFRICA

🍷 8 **Morrisons Pinotage 2013** £4.49
Value wine with discreet tarriness carried along by juicy-spicy verve and 14.5% alcohol. 'Brilliant with bangers', says the food-match note. Quite so.

🍷 9 **Signature South African Pinotage 2013** £6.99
Well-made typical pungent indigenous varietal is slick, spicy and rich with roasty character and nice balance, with 14.5% alcohol. Very fair price.

SPAIN

🍷 9 **Signature Navarra Garnacha 2012** £7.99
Muscular dark and sleek savoury varietal with a sprinkle of pepper and a clean grip of tannin with distinct Navarra (Rioja's southern neighbour) style; 14% alcohol.

🍷 7 **Signature Viña Eneldo Rioja Reserva 2007** £9.99
Plenty of vanilla and a middling allocation of fruit in this sweetly mature smoothie.

USA

🍷 8 **Lone Oak Merlot 2012** £12.99
Toffee-rich but artfully balanced black-cherry luxury Californian smoothie for roast chicken.

PINK WINES

8 **Amalthea Provence Rosé 2013** £8.99
Vanishingly pale coral colour to this fresh and delicately strawberry-sweet dry-finishing refresher.

8 **Sancerre Rosé 2013** £10.99
Show-off's wine from Pinot Noir, under an appellation really known for Sauvignon Blanc, has a discreet copper colour, raspberry-cherry Pinot fruit and a nice citrus twang.

7 **Morrisons Portuguese Rosé** £3.99
Can they sustain this price? A shocking-pink non-vintage near-spritzy redcurrant sweet-hit party pink with 10.5% alcohol.

8 **Signature Navarra Garnacha Rosé 2013** £7.99
Crisply fresh strawberry-nosed dry salmon-coloured wine has substance; 14% alcohol.

WHITE WINES

9 **Salentein Sauvignon Blanc 2013** £10.99
Whopper from Mendoza is dry and fresh, as well as expansive and deliciously expressive of the green-grass, glinty vivacity of the Sauvignon at the summit of its earthly powers. Yes, I liked it, a lot.

8 **Signature Grüner Veltliner 2013** £6.99
Crunchy orchard fruit and brassica figure in the aroma and flavour of this balanced dry herbaceous wine from the Niederösterreich.

WHITE WINES

CHILE

8 Signature Leyda Sauvignon Blanc 2013 £6.99
Eager gooseberry and nettle freshness to this Montgras-made fully fruity number.

8 LFE Marea Leyda Sauvignon Blanc 2013 £12.99
A jungle of exotic vegetal flavours issues from this grassy-fresh, brassica-crisp Luis Felipe Edwards serious-quality leesy wine with 14% alcohol; justifiable price.

FRANCE

8 La Sablette Muscadet 2013 £5.49
Cheap, inoffensive Loire-Atlantic shellfish bone-dry wine has gentle acidity.

8 Signature Premières Côtes de Bordeaux £6.49
Gloriously honeyed and golden-hued sweetie is delicately weighted and uncloying; great with puds, but also as an aperitif or with blue cheese.

8 Signature Touraine Sauvignon Blanc 2013 £6.99
Shiny bright and verdantly crisp Loire varietal on good form in a difficult vintage.

8 Picpoul de Pinet 2013 £7.99
Bright, defined and oyster-fresh Mediterranean refresher. Morrisons food-match advice includes 'surprisingly good with rich cheese and charcuterie'.

9 Signature Alsace Gewürztraminer 2012 £7.99
Plump lychee fruit follows the bunch-of-roses perfume in this on-target Gewürz from Türckheim co-op (where else?) with well-judged residual sugar; nice one at a better-than-usual price.

WHITE WINES

9 Signature Chablis 2011   £9.99
The first thing I like about this is that it tastes like Chablis.
You get the sweet-apple, oyster-shell, trace of spearmint,
gunflint aroma straight off, and full, generously ripe but
steely Chardonnay fruit in the mouth. Good minerality,
good wine.

9 Castelvero Bianco 2013   £4.99
Poor man's Gavi, made from the same grape, Cortese,
here with white fruit of perky crispness nicely balanced
with a creamy, blanched-almond richness; 11.5%
alcohol. A clever little cheapie made by artful Piedmont
mega-producer Araldica.

8 Signature Soave Classico 2013   £4.99
Cheap but recognisable Verona dry wine has crispness
and a hallmark touch of blanched almond richness;
11.5% alcohol.

8 Signature Gavi 2013   £5.99
Nice creamy-but-crisp classic Piedmont white at a keen
price.

8 Pecorino Abruzzo 2013   £7.99
Every supermarket has to have a Pecorino now, and this
one serves the purpose well. Ripe orchard fruit with
healthy sweetness finishing dry and clean.

8 Waikato River Sauvignon Blanc 2013   £6.99
Craftily contrived spearmint and seagrass Marlborough
wine includes small fractions of Chardonnay and Riesling.

WHITE WINES

 7 **Morrisons Vinho Verde** £4.49
Lightly sweet and faintly prickly non-vintage variation on
the green-wine theme is easy, unchallenging drinking with
just 8.5% alcohol.

10 **Signature Pedro Ximénez 37.5cl** £5.99
Conker colour, extravagant figgy fruitcake nose, gorgeous
currant, muscovado and roasted-nut richness make up the
series of sensations coalescing into the divine experience
of regarding, sniffing and sipping this miraculous fortified
wine from the white grape usually employed to sweeten
sherry; 17% alcohol. Bravo, Bodegas Emilio Lustau, for
making it, and Bravo, Morrisons, for offering it to its
discriminating customers.

8 **Signature Godello 2013** £7.99
Greengage was the fruit reference I noted cryptically for
this nuanced ripe but crisp rising varietal from Monterrei
in Galicia.

10 **Baron de Ley White Rioja Reserva 2008** £12.99
Not to everyone's taste, of course, but here's a fab
flashback to the Rioja Blanco of yesteryear. Gold colour,
oxidative tropical-fruit nose, creamy vanilla and lush
stone-fruit flavours of exciting liveliness and freshness, in
spite of the long ageing. A brilliant wine of its (all-too-
rare) kind for a Spanish feast of shellfish.

SPARKLING WINE

FRANCE

🍷 **8** **Signature Vintage Champagne 2007**   **£22.99**
Relatively young but developed single-vintage champagne
by Louis Kremer has creamy aroma, mouthfilling mousse
and fruit with a lemon zest.

Sainsbury's

Sainsbury's wine department is in a purple patch. The new vintages are the best I can remember over many years, and for the first time ever, some prices seem to be drifting gently lower.

I have been particularly impressed with some of the white wines from the difficult 2013 harvests in Europe. Last year was one of the most awkward vine-growing seasons across the Continent, mainly thanks to rain. There were downpours at all the wrong times, not just in Bordeaux and other French vinegrowing centres, but further south in Italy, Spain and Portugal too. Lack of sun as well as the wet in the spring inhibited flowering, and floods left vines standing in deep water in some very unexpected locations.

And yet there are some smashing new whites from France, Italy and Spain, even from Germany (very badly rain-affected) among the new Sainsbury's offering. As ever at Sainsbury's, the best wines are from the own-label ranges. The Winemakers' Selection wines, introduced only two years ago as a mid-price option between the basic 'House' products and the premium Taste the Difference range, already number more than 100. They are among the prime buys at Sainsbury's, and have, I'm sure, played a big part in lifting sales of own-brand wines by 16 per cent this year over last.

On the internet, Sainsbury's continues to confound me. There is no dedicated wine service of the kind run by all its main rivals, and it seems a long journey of clicks to find any wine in particular, let alone to order it.

That said, the stores are pleasant to shop in, and the wine discounts prodigious. There are regular promotions taking 25 per cent off the whole range, including wines already on generous individual discounts. These offers frequently coincide with similar deals at Tesco. Pure coincidence, no doubt.

RED WINES

ARGENTINA

9 **Winemakers' Selection Malbec 2013**   £4.75
A complete and generously ripe and balanced juicy-savoury blackberry-sweet food red with grip but not hardness, and all at a very low price indeed.

8 **Winemakers' Selection Australian
Petit Verdot 2013**   £5.00
Ripe-fruit healthy party red at a very keen price.

8 **Winemakers' Selection South Australian
Shiraz 2013**   £6.25
This does the job; sweetly ripe but trim-at-the-edge wholesome barbecue red.

AUSTRALIA

10 **DB Family Reserve Petite Sirah 2011**   £8.50
In a Riverina vintage year reportedly deluged by apocalyptic floods, the De Bortoli family has made a miraculous wine. The intense bitter black-cherry nose jumps out of the glass and the lush, complex, plummy-spicy fruit surges over the tastebuds. It's vital, vivid and utterly convincing, but very approachable indeed. Price is more than fair.

8 **Xanadu Next of Kin Cabernet Sauvignon
2011**   £8.50
Those drawn to loopy wine names might like to know that this Margaret River varietal is quite restrained in ripeness, almost claret-like, with quite elegantly balanced oaked blackcurrant fruit and 14% alcohol.

RED WINES

9 **Winemakers' Selection Costières de Nîmes 2012** £6.00

Plenty of spicy heart to the intense dark blackberry fruit of this characteristic Costières red from 50:50 Grenache and Syrah; smooth and rich, it's been made without oak and looks a bargain at this price.

9 **Taste the Difference Languedoc Red 2013** £8.00

Even in the tortured 2013 vintage this Jean-Claude Mas annual has triumphed: a soothingly substantial and spicy oaked food red with great balance; 14% alcohol.

10 **Château la Tulipe de la Garde 2011** £10.00

This estate near St Emilion had the prosaic name La Garde until Dutch owner Ilja Gort added the Tulipe (geddit?) in 2010. The Merlot-dominated wine, though ranked a mere Bordeaux Supérieur, is simply gorgeous, deep, blood red and roundly ripe with 14% alcohol. Gort claims his 2011 benefits from the serenades his singing Dutch pickers gave the grapes at harvest.

8 **Chapoutier Crozes Hermitage Les Meysonniers 2011** £16.00

Pale pure Syrah from northern Rhône has a lemony twang atop the typical strawberry-prune fruit; good of its kind, but needs a couple more years in bottle.

9 **Louis Max Côtes de Nuits Villages 2012** £18.00

Utterly delicious burgundy of purity and silkiness already drinking well; pale and glowing partridge-eye colour and a heavenly cherry-strawberry nose; really quite good value at this price.

RED WINES

ITALY

🍷 9 **Taste the Difference Barbaresco 2010** £10.00
Gently browning colour, sweet-cherry-and-cold-tea nose and a slinky cherry-spice fruit combine to form a convincing introduction to a classic and usually expensive Piedmont wine style; 14% alcohol.

🍷 9 **Torre de Mastio Amarone della Valpolicella Classico 2009** £23.00
Epic conker-deep crimson-coloured Verona speciality wine has a rich black-cherry-liqueur nose and liquorice-hearted porty weight, all in fine balance with the dry amarone bitterness giving a lipsmacking end; 15% alcohol.

N. ZEALAND

🍷 8 **Taste the Difference Central Otago Pinot Noir 2012** £11.00
Pale but perky, cherry-raspberry, immediately recognisable Kiwi Pinot with punchy, crisp and fresh impact will chill nicely; 14% alcohol.

PORTUGAL

🍷 8 **Winemakers' Selection Portuguese Red** £5.00
Sardine-on-the barbecue juicy, clovey, proper Portuguese sinewy-minty bargain red.

🍷 8 **Taste the Difference Douro 2012** £8.50
From table-wine specialist Quinta do Crasto (est. 1615), a nice clingy-minty black-fruit slicker with porty nose and an easy weight; 14% alcohol.

SPAIN

🍷 8 **Winemakers' Selection Rioja Reciente** £5.25
Non-vintage Rioja is a rare bird, but this has the authentic sweetly oaked midweight strawberry-blackcurrant fruitiness, and an alluring price.

RED WINES

8 Pasico Old Vine Monastrell Shiraz 2013   £6.00
Deep purple, briar-ripe food red from Jumilla has masses
of savoury black fruit with a gripping, lipsmacking finish.

**7 Winemakers' Selection Cariñena
Gran Reserva 2008**   £6.00
Pale-looking old Rioja-pretender has curiosity value for
its fading sweet mellowness.

**8 Taste the Difference Cepa Alegro
Rioja Reserva 2008**   £10.00
Earthy, truffly notes to the ripe strawberry and vanilla in
this sheeny, sleek and vigorous mature Rioja.

8 Taste the Difference Priorat 2011   £11.00
The best so far of this economy Priorat, darkly intense
and toasty-oaked keeping red with 14.5% alcohol.

**9 Condado de Haza Crianza Ribera del Duero
2010**   £17.00
Tarry-coloured pure Tempranillo has long, toothsome,
plummy black-fruit savour with a seductive baked
richness highlighted by spices and mint; gorgeous special-
occasion wine of a prestige region; 14.5% alcohol.

PINK WINES

**9 Winemakers' Selection Australian Shiraz
Sangiovese Rosé 2013**   £4.75
I don't know who dreams up these grape blends, but
this party-frock-pink combo works wonders of perky
freshness and crisp summer-soft-fruit juiciness; very dry
and very cheap.

PINK WINES

 Winemakers' Selection Chilean Cabernet Sauvignon Rosé 2013 £6.00

Dignified pale onion-skin colour, a whiff of cassis and a fairly intense crisp blackcurrant fruitiness make this a rosé to be reckoned with; food wine.

 Winemakers' Selection Côtes du Rhône Rosé 2013 £6.00

Dry bordering on austere, crispy but juicy Mediterranean pink with freshness.

Taste the Difference Côtes de Provence Rosé 2013 £8.00

Pale shell-pink colour, pretty dry and prettily presented stawberry-juice fresh summer wine.

Winemakers' Selection Fairtrade Pinotage Rosé 2013 £6.50

Attractive smoked-salmon colour, floral whiff, full-fruited but dry-finishing and interesting refresher.

WHITE WINES

 Winemakers' Selection Limestone Coast Chardonnay 2012 £6.00

Nostalgic yellow oaked apple-pie Chardy happens to be wholesomely balanced and brightly lively. It's rare to find good Aussie wine at this sort of price these days.

Fairbank Semillon 2013 £9.00

Peach, melon and possibly guava feature in this fruit-salad varietal (with a bit of Chardonnay added) from Riverland, all coalescing into a lushly exotic, discreetly oaked dry food wine: roast chicken as well as fishy dishes.

WHITE WINES

8 **Pocketwatch Chardonnay 2013** £10.00
Rich and creamy with sweet vanilla notes to the ripe
peachy-appley fruit and a brisk lemon edge; from
Mudgee, New South Wales.

8 **Peter Lehmann Portrait Barossa
Chardonnay 2012** £11.25
Iconic wine with clean attack, lush varietal ripeness and
richness, and elegant balance.

8 **Taste the Difference Grüner Veltliner 2013** £7.50
Dry but pungent varietal (Austria's most widely planted)
has a floral nose, spicy white fruit with notes of sage and
clove; distinctive wine to match white meats, fish, salads
– you name it.

8 **Winemakers' Selection Côtes de Gascogne
2013** £6.00
Green grassy nose and familiar Sauvignon fruit followed
by a lemon lift make this edgy dry white from south-west
France taste more interesting than its vague provenance
might promise.

8 **Taste the Difference Muscadet
Sèvre et Maine Sur Lie 2013** £7.00
Unanticipated ripe melon aroma, but a pleasantly tangy
and seagrass-fresh bone-dry shellfish white.

9 **Picpoul de Pinet 2013** £8.00
Brisk, lemony and abounding with eager orchard fruit,
this is a particularly lively variation on a now-fashionable
Mediterranean theme.

WHITE WINES

8 **Taste the Difference Gewürztraminer 2013** **£8.00**
Sweet bloom of rose perfume and lots of lychee pungency
in this balanced, off-dry aperitif; proper Alsace Gewürz,
not oversweet.

10 **Taste the Difference Languedoc White 2013** **£8.00**
It's a pound cheaper than the delectable 2012 and the same
artful contrivance of richness, orchard-fruit crispness and
tingling citrus tang, from the magic formula of Marsanne
and Grenache Blanc plus Vermentino by ubiquitous Jean-
Claude Mas. Blandly named, maybe, but a flagship own-
label for Sainsbury's.

8 **Château le Bernet Graves Blanc 2013** **£9.00**
Fun double act of tropical fruit and briny, nettly freshness
works well in this dry, racy Bordeaux.

9 **Sancerre Les Caillottes 2013** **£12.00**
Authentic stony-gunflint aroma from this vivid Loire
Sauvignon bears witness to the 'caillotte' stones that
populate the limestone-clay vineyards; a smashing wine,
realistically priced.

9 **Taste the Difference Pouilly Fumé 2013** **£12.00**
Lemon-gold colour, exotic green-fruit perfume and flinty
purity of lush Sauvignon fruit mark out this perennial
Loire classic, finishing with a lick of leesy richness beside
the citrus-keen finish.

8 **Chablis Premier Cru Selection**
Domaines Brocard 2012 **£16.00**
Gold colour in which it is easy to imagine the proverbial
green highlights, and lavish-but-flinty proper Chablis
Chardonnay purity; exciting quality at a price.

WHITE WINES

GERMANY

🍷 9 **Dr L Riesling 2013** £7.50
So fresh, tingly and crisp it's almost spritzy, this is a delicious apple-sweet, delicately balanced moselle of great character, and just 8.5% alcohol. Another outstanding vintage from Germany's star winemaker.

ITALY

🍷 9 **Winemakers' Selection Fiano 2013** £5.25
The cheapest Fiano on the market and by no means the least likeable I have tasted, this has perky, crunchy fruit with length and balance; from Salento, a thoroughly Italian dry white to match creamy or fishy pastas.

🍷 8 **Winemakers' Selection Gavi 2013** £6.50
Crisp but nuanced nuts-and-apples dry Piedmont white currently in fashion has a whisper of creaminess and a modest 11.5% alcohol. Good price.

🍷 9 **Taste the Difference Greco di Tufo 2012** £9.00
Beautifully presented Campania wine is still the vintage from last year. Why hasn't it sold out? The gold colour might be a little more so, but the plush white orchard fruit and zesty citrus twang are as plush and twangy as ever. A great food white that last year was priced at £10.49.

N. ZEALAND

🍷 8 **Winemakers' Selection Marlborough Chardonnay 2012** £7.75
Kiwi Chardonnay doesn't get much of a look-in, but here's a nice generously lush one with a lick of oak vanilla, comforting plumpness, a sensible price and a style of its own.

WHITE WINES

NEW ZEALAND

9 Taste the Difference Awatere Valley
Riesling 2013   £8.50
Love this limey sour-apple stimulating food white for its
sheer zest, the Riesling character coming confidently into
play as you savour its ideal weight and balance; made by
esteemed Yealands Estate at 11.5% alcohol.

10 Taste the Difference Riverblock
Marlborough Sauvignon Blanc 2013   £11.00
I hear so much whingeing from my wine-writing
colleagues about the uniformity of Kiwi Sauvignon these
days that I rather hesitate to go wild over yet another
own-brand. Well, I love this one. It has a good rasp of
edgy citrus acidity, a mad salad of Sauvignon sensations
– asparagus, nettles, seagrass, french beans, pyracantha
(oh, all right, I made that last one up) – and a transcending
joyful vivacity that is wholly irresistible.

PORTUGAL

7 Winemakers' Selection Vinho Verde   £4.75
Yellow, prickly, sweet, fruit-juicy, shamelessly commercial
non-vintage party variation on the bone-dry true Vinho
Verde theme; 9% alcohol.

S. AFRICA

9 Zalze Reserve Chenin Blanc 2012   £10.00
The nose put me in mind of banana custard. It's a dry
wine, mind you, fresh and stimulating, but also rich with
ripe melon flavours and a creamy luxuriance. Chenin
seems to have a unique capacity for unexpectedly thrilling
counterpoint.

SPAIN

8 Taste the Difference Albariño 2013   £8.25
Consistent Rias Baixas (Atlantic north-west) pure varietal
is seaside fresh and bracing with long white-fruit flavours.

SPARKLING WINES

10 Sainsbury's Blanc de Noirs Champagne Brut £22.25

Perennial favourite from six parts Pinot Meunier to four Pinot Noir is distinctively made with digestive-biscuit perfume, mellow, lively and long fruit, and a sense of careful upbringing; special quality at an occasionally madly reduced price. In 2014 I bought a magnum for £26.25 – the champagne bargain of the year.

8 Sainsbury's Demi-Sec Champagne £22.50

'Demi-Sec' in champagne-speak means sweet, but this one is more soft and creamy than sugary, and entirely lacking the green acidity that can upset those unaccustomed to champagne; nice product.

Tesco

I loved the headline that greeted one of Tesco's recent run of trading dips: 'Profits plunge to £3.3bn.'

It says it all, really. Tesco is gigantic, so any downturn in its fortunes calls for a gloat. But look at it this way: Tesco is Britain's largest private-sector employer. Lots of able and good-hearted people work there.

Quite a few of them are to be found in the wine department. The ones I encounter at tastings bear little resemblance to the ravening profiteers you might expect from the media coverage. They are enthusiastic and professional when it comes to discussing the wines. The interests of customers are uppermost.

The wines bear it out. Most of those I have picked out for this report are from Tesco's flagship 'Finest' own-label range. They are unique to Tesco and many are made with input from the wine team. Value is consistently fair, and yet these wines feature regularly in Tesco's perpetual price promotions. These can make some very sound wines look insanely cheap.

There are now more than 100 Finest wines, but they still account for a mere fraction of the entire choice at Tesco. Most of the shelf space in the stores is still given over to the familiar global brands, dominated by Australia, California and South Africa. These continue to account for the great bulk of sales, not just at Tesco but across the whole retail sector.

My advice is to pay them no attention. The real interest and value at Tesco is seriously concentrated in its own-label wines and in a few individual brands from the more quality-driven kind of producer on the Continent and – occasionally – in the southern hemisphere.

The width of the wine range varies wildly according to the size and rating of individual stores. For the biggest guaranteed choice, look online. Tesco has the best wine website of the lot, and it delivers the next day.

RED WINES

ARGENTINA

8 Finest Argentina Malbec 2013 £7.99
Likeably austere Catena wine doesn't stint on ripe fruit and spicy savour.

AUSTRALIA

10 Sister's Run Barossa Cabernet Sauvignon 2011 £8.00
Blood-red friendly monster has ballerina-poised balance between pure, vivid cassis Cabernet fruit and eager but gentle tannin grip to finish the long flavour rush; 14% alcohol. This is a jump-out Aussie wine and a rare bargain. Online by the case only.

8 Sister's Run Barossa Grenache 2012 £8.00
Raspberry nose is unexpectedly followed by a more rustic briar-berry fruit; bright, pale-coloured and intriguingly poised, with 14.5% alcohol. Online by the case only.

8 McGuigan The Shortlist GSM 2010 £15.00
Eight parts Grenache to two of Shiraz and Mourvèdre, a light-touch, spicy-juicy Barossa with richness and balance. Online by the case only.

CHILE

8 Luis Felipe Edwards Vintage Selection Shiraz 2012 £4.89
Artful cheapie is not short on fruit, and finishes clean and bright.

8 Montes Reserva Cabernet Sauvignon 2012 £7.49
Pleasingly defined cassis fruit in this toffee-rich (but unoaked) and clean-finishing balanced juicy red; 14% alcohol.

RED WINES

Tesco

CHILE

9 **Casillero del Diablo Devil's Collection Red 2012** £8.99

Plush package for this muscular, spicy oaked red from infallible Concha y Toro; Syrah-based blend of real character.

9 **Concha y Toro Marques de Casa Concha Syrah 2011** £11.99

The creaminess of the new oak by no means overwhelms the high-toned, pure, lush, spicy Syrah fruit in this intense, purple-black luxury wine to match meaty menus; 14.5% alcohol.

FRANCE

8 **Labrune Pinot Noir 2013** £5.99

Intensely coloured Loire-based red has a Beaujolais-like bounce to the soft summer fruit and a crisp edge.

9 **Tesco Beaujolais-Villages 2013** £6.49

Lively raspberry perfume leaps from the glass; the fruit is soft and easy but not short on juiciness or crispness; bodes well for the vintage.

9 **Finest Côtes Catalanes Carignan 2012** £7.49

Companion wine to the outstanding Grenache below, this dense, briary and spicy Pyrenean red has a lot of rugged southern charm. Again, a frequent discount attraction.

10 **Finest Côtes Catalanes Grenache 2013** £7.49

Dark, brambly Perpignan varietal is now a perennial favourite, regularly discounted from a perfectly reasonable standard price, and providing nourishing, dark, spicy flavours in ideal balance. I can think of no more dependable wine on the market so often available at around, or even under, a fiver.

RED WINES

8 **Château La Hitte Buzet 2012** £10.00
Amusingly named Merlot-Cabernets mix from obscure
Gascon appellation Buzet has deep purple colour and
plenty of spicy, grippy briar fruit; healthy and invigorating.
Online by the case only.

8 **Finest Gigondas 2012** £12.99
I'm still hankering for a reprise of the fabled 2007 vintage
of this grand Rhône red. This part-oaked, dense and
savoury effort will make a reasonable stop-gap; 14%
alcohol.

8 **Finest Nuits St Georges 2012** £19.99
Here you are: a twenty-quid supermarket burgundy
worth the money; light in colour but with a big, rich,
sun-kissed Pinot Noir nose and intense, expensive-tasting
grippy fruit in good balance.

9 **Finest Margaux 2008** £24.99
Premium own-label Bordeaux by famed Château
d'Angludet has heavenly Margaux perfume and plump,
rich fruit in perfect balance. Proper claret nicely presented
at an almost-forgivable price; in only 42 selected stores.

6 **Château Pichon Longueville**
Comtesse de Lalande 2009 £140.00
From Tesco's hoard of classed-growth clarets of the
legendary 2009 vintage, a top name with nice ruby
colour, inscrutable nose and promising pruny-tobacco
fruit in need of many more years in bottle. Online by the
case (£840) only.

FRANCE

RED WINES

FRANCE

7 Château Pontet-Canet 2009 £150.00
Another from the Tesco claret treasury, this time already lovely to taste, dark and dense with a lifted plummy-cedar-cassis fruit and creamy silkiness on which the tannin is easing its grip; 14% alcohol. Ridiculously expensive. Online by the case only.

8 Colpasso Nero d'Avola Terre Siciliane 2012 £6.50
Eye-catching label and perpetual online discounting are additional lures to this dark, pungent, sunnily ripe pizza red. Online by the case only.

8 Finest Frappato 2012 £7.99
Juicy, bouncing, summer-soft-fruit Sicilian red has the same feel (but different fruit) as Beaujolais. Will repay time spent in the fridge. Vigorous, charming and dry-finishing, a good match for oily fish and salad days.

ITALY

9 Finest Teroldego 2012 £7.99
Another wizard vintage for this bold sub-Alpine varietal, dark purple-crimson with a sweet but spiky nose, lipsmacking black-fruit flavours with minty, leafy notes and a crisp finish.

9 Lava Beneventano Aglianico 2010 £9.79
I am a sucker for the monster black volcanic wines of the Campania, especially when made from the Aglianico grape; this artfully packaged rugged roast-matcher has core flavours of dark chocolate and even coffee amid intense black-cherry fruit, finishing beautifully dry and lipsmacking.

RED WINES

ITALY

🍷 9 **Finest Barolo 2010**   **£15.99**
First time this wine has registered with me since the 2005 vintage, which was made, like this one, by the good people at Ascheri. Handsome ruby colour going orange, exotic spirity-sappy nose, lashings of typical sleek fruit. The real thing, drinking well now; 14% alcohol.

N. ZEALAND

🍷 8 **Villa Maria Reserve Pinot Noir 2010**   **£17.99**
Seductively ripe and plump Kiwi classic for special occasions, including festive roast birds.

PORTUGAL

🍷 8 **Finest Vinha do Vinteiro Douro Reserve 2011**   **£19.99**
Gorgeous red wine from the port country is suitably dark and soupy with clinging black fruits and firm but friendly tannins with lush mint and spice; you get the comfort of port without the sweetness and alcohol (though this does have 14%).

SOUTH AFRICA

🍷 8 **Quirky Bird Shiraz Mourvèdre Viognier 2013**   **£6.99**
Roasty rounded gently spicy typical Cape red to match chilli dishes; 14% alcohol.

🍷 9 **Bellingham The Bernard Series Basket Press Syrah 2012**   **£10.99**
Untypical of the Cape, I thought, but a deliciously defined Syrah with expensive new-oak smoothness and intensity; 14% alcohol. Biggest stores only.

RED WINES

SPAIN

🍷 **8** **Simply Garnacha** £4.79

Straight briar-spice, very dry-finishing but generously fruity non-vintage bargain.

🍷 **9** **Gran Fabrica Cariñena Gran Reserva 2006** £6.00

Artful oaked Rioja-lite style with a nice minty savour was £36.00 per six online at time of tasting, and as such, a great bargain.

🍷 **10** **Finest Viña Mara Rioja Gran Reserva 2007** £11.49

Huge improvement on dried-out 2004 vintage, there's no sign of browning; a big sweet-vanilla youthfully vigorous but evolved rich ripeness here, with a nice tug of tannin. Pure Tempranillo matured in new oak.

USA

🍷 **8** **Primarius Oregon Pinot Noir 2011** £8.99

Almost alarmingly pale, this brisk, cool-climate, strawberry-ripe Pinot is nevertheless compellingly defined and long flavoured.

PINK WINES

ARGENTINA

🍷 **8** **Finest Argentina Malbec Rosé 2013** £7.99
Pale but interesting Catena-made dry-finishing brisk briar-fruit refresher is self-evidently well-made.

FRANCE

🍷 **8** **Tesco Vin de France Rosé** £4.49
Pale salmon, inoffensive strawberry-style, non-vintage dry party pink has a crafty lick of sweetness; Gamay-Merlot, 11% alcohol and very cheap.

🍷 **8** **Finest Domaine de Sours Rosé 2013** £6.79
Ubiquitous and consistent Bordeaux pink has the cherry appeal of its constituent Merlot fruit; clean, crisp and classy at the price.

ITALY

🍷 **7** **Finest Nero d'Avola Rosé 2013** £7.99
Perennial pink from Sicily's giant Cantine Settesoli has Ribena colour and lots of grippy dry briary fruit; not cheap.

SPAIN

🍷 **8** **Simply Garnacha Rosé** £4.59
Boldly coloured Campo de Borja non-vintage has a good slurp of summer soft fruit and stimulating dry style, as well as the alluring price.

🍷 **8** **Revero Rosé** £4.99
Lured by the nice label, I couldn't help liking this perky blackcurranty Extremadura Tempranillo non-vintage dry-finishing bargain; 11% alcohol.

🍷 **8** **Finest Viña Mara Rioja Rosado 2013** £7.99
Onion-skin colour and big flavours from this heady dry wine from the traditional Rioja mix of Tempranillo and Garnacha grapes.

WHITE WINES

8 **Finest Argentina Chardonnay 2013** £8.49
Yellow in colour, hint of butter (though no oak) in the ripe-apple richness; dry, fresh wine made by Catena, and it shows.

8 **Finest Argentina Torrontes 2013** £8.99
Like the Chardonnay above, it's by Catena, and amply exhibits the distinct Muscat-grape sweet spiciness that is the Torrontes signature; a fine aperitif wine that contrives to be both rich and crisp.

8 **McWilliams Mount Pleasant Elizabeth Semillon 2006** £8.99
Yellow, oxidative, tropical but dry fascinator from New South Wales will make an exotic match for seafood; I love it, but it's an acquired taste, and just 10.5% alcohol.

9 **Tim Adams Protégé Clare Valley Riesling 2010** £9.50
Perfect poise and length to this textbook limey dry Riesling in the Aussie manner, with an irresistible lick of richness. Online by the case only.

8 **Finest Boranup Sauvignon Blanc Semillon 2012** £9.99
Bordeaux-themed blend makes a pungent and convincing dry wine for summer drinking; elegant refreshment.

10 **McGuigan The Shortlist Chardonnay 2011** £15.00
I carefully compared this to Tesco's £20 Meursault and preferred it by a mile; luscious, de luxe, new-oak-fermented, beautifully balanced Chardy of huge character. Online by the case only – invest with confidence.

WHITE WINES

8 McGuigan The Shortlist Riesling 2012   £15.00
Limey, racy, lush shellfish partner in the grand style that
will, says the back label, reward cellaring for 5+ years.
Invest now. It's 11.5% alcohol and online by the case
only.

**8 Luis Felipe Edwards Vintage Selection
Sauvignon Blanc 2013   £4.89**
Workmanlike bargain dry wine adds tropical, typically
Chilean, notes to the familiar gooseberry zest.

**8 Casillero del Diablo Devil's Collection
White 2012   £8.99**
Concha y Toro is at risk of overplaying its Devil card,
but this mainly Sauvignon plush dry white is refreshingly
interesting and broadly appealing.

8 Lucien Marcel Vin de Pays du Gers 2013   £5.99
Rather niftily balanced aromatic-tangy dry aperitif wine
from a region not always renowned for quality has an
intriguing beeswax whiff and lemon zest finish; 11.5%
alcohol.

8 Tesco Mâcon Blanc Villages 2013   £6.49
Likeable brassica whiff from this mineral, apple-peach
Chardonnay by ubiquitous Blason de Bourgogne brand.

9 Finest Saint Mont 2012   £6.99
Perennial Pyrenean favourite is vividly fresh as well as
ripely lush in the best fruit-salad sort of way; lots of
colour, aroma and nuance of flavour. A food wine to
match poultry, charcuterie or starchy dishes as well as
fish.

WHITE WINES

8 **Finest Château Palatio Muscadet Sèvre et Maine Sur Lie 2013** £7.49
Crisp and tangy Loire classic has plenty of leesy fruit; it can be rather challenging, acidity-wise, but this one is friendly rather than fierce, and grows on you; 11% alcohol.

8 **Finest Picpoul de Pinet 2013** £7.99
Pleasant, piquant Mediterranean dry white has become fashionable, but try it anyway.

8 **Finest Limoux Chardonnay 2011** £8.49
Curiosity from the Atlantic south-west has sweet-apple ripeness and creamy richness alongside abounding freshness and tang. Delightful.

8 **Château Loustalet Buzet 2012** £10.00
From the remote Gascon appellation of Buzet, a rare dry white in the Bordeaux style; ripe, plump white fruit with a grassy lushness and crispness. Online by the case only.

9 **Finest Sancerre 2013** £10.49
The Loire's prestige appellation for Sauvignon Blanc is fighting back well against the Kiwi tide. This stony-fresh, springwater-pure wine by good outfit Fournier has ripeness and gravitas, and it's competitively priced.

8 **Finest Pouilly-Fumé 2013** £11.99
Second in celebrity only to Sancerre in the Loire, this Sauvignon genuinely has a smoky aroma (ref. the Fumé in the name) reminiscent of struck gunflint. Lovely wine.

WHITE WINES

 **8 St Stephan's Crown Tokaji Aszu 5 Puttonyos 2008 50cl** £15.00
Ambrosial copper-gold stickie from the eternally mysterious Tokay vineyards of the Bodrog Valley has Sauternes-like richness and balance; 11.5% alcohol. Online by the case only.

8 Finest Fiano 2013 £7.99
Ubiquitous own-brand stocked in 2,576 Tesco stores sells more than a million bottles a year. It's a generously coloured, orchard-fruit dry wine with a lick of almond richness, from Sicily.

10 Finest Gavi 2013 £7.99
This is outstanding: a lushly developed dry wine drawing on crisp apples and sweet pears for the inspiration for its intriguing flavours. It's pale to look at but weighty with blanched-almond richness and finished with a limey edge. From Cortese grapes grown in the misty vineyards of Piedmont.

8 Finest Soave Classico Superiore 2012 £7.99
A long way from the usual weedy branded stuff, this is a committed, ripely fruity, proper Soave with plush white fruit, nutty fullness and keen citrus edge. Satisfying.

8 Finest Dolomiti Chardonnay 2011 £14.99
Unexpected vanilla-oaked but restrained Trentino dry white with minerality and peachy Chardonnay lushness in artful balance; 14% alcohol. Biggest stores only.

WHITE WINES

8 NZSB Marlborough Sauvignon Blanc 2013 £7.49
From pioneering Babich winery, this has zip and agreeable greenness to balance ripe and sunny fruit.

10 Finest Awatere Valley Pinot Grigio 2012 £7.99
If you must drink Pinot Grigio, drink this. It's a gorgeous, ripe, smoky, just-off-dry wine rather in the Alsace Pinot Gris style, with spicy notes and long herbaceous flavours. Made by starry Yealands Estate in Marlborough, a grand aperitif and versatile food white.

8 Finest North Row Vineyard Sauvignon Blanc 2013 £14.99
Zingy, grassy-gooseberry, intensely focused Marlborough wine from new Tesco premium range is made by Villa Maria. Lovely wine, a little expensive.

7 Tesco Vinho Verde £4.59
Softened but not quite sweet non-vintage spin on the admirable 'green wine' style has a lift of tanginess and 11% alcohol.

7 Finest Vinho Verde 2013 £7.49
Interesting apple perfume, signs of crispness; 11.5% alcohol.

9 Finest Stellenbosch Sauvignon Blanc 2013 £9.99
The magic word is Vergelegen, one of the Cape's best (if least pronounceable) estates. They've made a stonking wine for Tesco, bursting with gooseberry ripeness, awash with grassy lushness, enriched with a small shot of Semillon and 14% alcohol.

WHITE WINES

SPAIN

🍷 8 **Finest Albariño 2013**   £7.49
From famed Galician co-op Martin Codax, a clean, crisp
example of this cult wine at a good price.

USA

🍷 8 **Washington Hills Riesling 2011**   £8.99
Ethereal, appley, pleasantly fruit-juicy style to this delicate
aperitif from the American north-west; 11.5% alcohol.

SPARKLING WINES

BRAZIL

7 **I Heart Brasil Sparkling Moscato** £9.99
World Cup/Olympics gimmick is distinctly akin to Asti
Spumante. Pretty sweet and 8.5% alcohol.

FRANCE

9 **Leprince Royer Champagne Brut** £15.00
Lots of bright freshness but no trace of greenness in this
foolishly named anonymous brand at a very keen price.
Online by the case only.

9 **Finest Premier Cru Champagne Brut** £19.99
Impressively consistent Chardonnay-dominated
champagne from well-rated vineyards has reassuring gold
colour, lemon-and-digestive-bikky perfume and long,
satisfying flavours.

9 **Finest Vintage Champagne Grand Cru
Brut 2007** £24.99
Lots of colour and bready yeastiness on the nose of this
pure-Chardonnay, mature and developed wine from top-
rated vineyards; lovely now and will repay keeping for as
long as you can bear it.

ITALY

7 **Simply Prosecco** £6.99
Pale colour, pear-juice nose and matching fruit finishes
just shy of dry. Gentle mousse and 11% alcohol.

8 **InVilla Prosecco Brut** £7.50
Elaborately bottled dry-style has lively mousse, attractive
white-fruit and acidity balance with a lemon twang; 11%
alcohol. Online by the case only.

Waitrose

 Waitrose seems set on world domination. In the 2005 edition of this book, I reported that the store network had in the preceding year expanded from 144 to 163. Waitrose starts 2015, according to chief wine buyer Pierpaolo Petrassi, with 342 branches.

There is no reason to suppose that bigger means better, of course, but in Waitrose's case it certainly makes it likelier than ever that there's a store not far from where you live.

The wine range hasn't suffered at all, as far as I can see. Every branch I have visited has had a formidable selection from the 1,000-plus wines listed overall, and less shelf space is given over to dull global brands than elsewhere.

Waitrose is very gradually building up its range of own-label wines. I guess this process will gather momentum as the number of outlets increases. To sell own-brands you do, after all, need to have a realistically large network.

In that case, bigger will mean better at Waitrose, because the own-label wines so far look very good. I particularly commend the lately introduced basic generic range. Waitrose Mellow and Fruity Spanish Red 2013 at £4.99 is phenomenally good for the money.

Sheer choice is the main attraction, as ever. Many of the wines are exclusive, prices are entirely competitive (they always have been) and yet dramatic discounting is not a ploy Waitrose considers beneath its dignity. This is a place for bargains.

Online, there has been a change. Out goes Waitrose Wine Direct. In comes Waitrose Cellar. It all looks like window dressing to me. But you still get a vast choice, a reasonably clear website and free delivery within three working days.

RED WINES

8 **Waitrose Argentinian Malbec 2013** £8.99
Friendly rendering of the national grape delivers dark savour and easy weight, all in healthy natural balance; 14% alcohol.

9 **Norton Winemaker's Reserve Malbec 2011** £11.99
Big beefy pure varietal stands out from the ever-growing Mendoza Malbec crowd; creamy-toasty oak flatters rather than masks the vigorous black fruit and it wears the 14.5% alcohol lightly.

9 **Clos de los Siete 2011** £15.99
Benchmark Mendoza luxury blend of mostly Malbec – with a bunch of other Bordeaux-origin varieties plus Syrah – is superb in this new vintage, cushiony with plump and creamy black fruits but trim, brisk and focused in its gentle grip and balancing acidity, with 14.5% alcohol. If it seems to resemble the elegant claret style, blame estate co-owner and winemaker Michel Rolland, a celebrity Bordeaux oenologist.

ARGENTINA

8 **Deakin Estate Vine Series Merlot 2013** £8.99
Straightforward black-cherry Victoria wine with likeable raspy vigour.

AUSTRALIA

8 **Luis Felipe Edwards Carmenère/Shiraz 2013** £5.99
Dark and easy smoothie with long savour, good balance and agreeable spiciness.

CHILE

RED WINES

CHILE

🍷 8 **Tabali Encantado Reserva Shiraz 2012**   £11.49
Purply-black colour and a coaly-roasty centre to the sunny-ripe black fruit in this Limari Valley Sunday-roast red; 14% alcohol.

FRANCE

🍷 8 **Esprit des Trois Pierres Costières de Nîmes 2013**   £7.79
Dark, roasty-pruny comfortingly familiar spicy Costières has proper southern savour and 14% alcohol.

🍷 8 **Bijou Cuvée Sophie Valrose Cabrières 2012** £7.99
Nothing bijou about this oaked blackberry Syrah-Grenache Mediterranean blend that has sweet ripeness and spice in sunny counterpoint, and 14% alcohol.

🍷 8 **Waitrose Southern French Grenache 2013**   £7.99
Pure varietal Pays d'Oc is full of heart, spicy and grippy with that indefinable garrigue savour of the Gard.

🍷 8 **Château de Caraguilhes Corbières 2012**   £9.99
Old friend from the hothouse Mediterranean appellation of Corbières is unexpectedly restrained and elegant in its supple, Syrah-based fruit, made without oak; 14% alcohol.

🍷 10 **Cave de Roquebrun Col de la Serre St Chinian 2012**   £10.99
Deep purple, plummy-spicy, delightfully abrading typical St Chinian of arresting character has a style unique in Languedoc, perhaps due to unusual Carignan-led blend, with Grenache, Syrah and Mourvèdre. Intense and peppery but sublimely balanced. Online from Waitrose Cellar only (more's the pity).

RED WINES

8   **Château de la Cour d'Argent 2011**   **£10.99**
Dramatically deep purple colour and liquorice depths to this Merlot-dominated Bordeaux Supérieur resolve in a satisfying ripe and generous 'modern' claret of healthy savour.

8   **Les Complices de Loire Les Graviers Chinon 2012**   **£10.99**
Bright purple, crisply leafy, juicy Loire red has violet perfume and relishable redcurrant fruit; a really outstanding style that deserves more recognition, and chills nicely too.

8   **Château de Chénas Moulin à Vent 2011**   **£11.99**
The label helpfully points out that this is a Cru Beaujolais, and it's a great one, juicy with Gamay bounce and weighty with ripe sunny fruit and a fine refreshing abrasion.

8   **Joseph Drouhin Chorey-lès-Beaune 2012**   **£15.99**
Fancy burgundy with earthy-farmyardy sinfully sleek Pinot Noir plumpness; you get what you pay for.

9   **Karl Heinz Johner Enselberg Pinot Noir 2009**   **£19.99**
Now would you seriously pick this Baden beauty out of the Waitrose posh-wine section (three megastores or online only)? You wouldn't be disappointed. Lovely lifting strawberry nose, gorgeous pure wildly ripe cool-climate Pinot of a kind entirely its own; 14% alcohol.

FRANCE

GERMANY

RED WINES

GREECE

9 Tsantali Organic Cabernet Sauvignon 2011 £9.49
From (Greek) Macedonian resort of Halkidiki, a lush, healthy cassis-and-cedar part-new-oaked claretty Cabernet of extraordinary purity and balance, and 14% alcohol. What a find.

ITALY

8 Recchia Bardolino 2013 £7.99
Unfortunate name but a nice almond-and-cherry-scented midweight pale red with some guts; a dry antipasto wine that will chill well.

9 Araldica Barbera d'Asti Superiore 2011 £8.99
'Superiore' does signify: it means three years' ageing and a minimum 13% alcohol; this vigorously juicy and intense blueberry bouncer certainly qualifies, with its sleek oak contact and 14.5% alcohol; de luxe and fun.

9 Paolo Leo Primitivo di Manduria 2011 £10.99
Black-as-night Puglian has wholesome prune-coffee-bitter-chocolate centre to the grippy, spicy very dry-finishing fruit. Great sticky meaty pasta match; 14.5% alcohol.

8 Masi Campofiorin 2010 £12.99
Iconic Veronese double-ferment red on the Ripasso Valpolicella model is a mellow, nutty, even raisiny dark velvet wine with notions of cloves and cinnamon, oak-aged for 18 months; I have happily bought this on discount over the year; at under a tenner it scores 9.

8 Oddero Barolo 2009 £23.99
Silkily developed, gently browning, sleek bitter-cherry and sweet-plum luxury classic with 14.5% alcohol. Safe investment.

RED WINES

 Ca'Bertoldi Amarone della Valpolicella
Classico 2007 £34.99

A disinterested joy to taste rare wine like this, which is simply gorgeous in all the right ways; 16.5% alcohol. Buy it if you can afford it. This has been a public service announcement.

 Seifried Estate Nelson Bay Pinot Noir
2011 £12.99

Colour's just north of rosé in this poised strawberry-cherry earthy sleek characteristic Kiwi Pinot.

 Craggy Range Gimblett Gravels Vineyard
Merlot 2010 £16.99

A unique Kiwi spin on the Merlot delivers this Hawke's Bay prodigy of rich but tight fruit with luxurious plumpness and poise; nothing like the Bordeaux right-bank version, but decidedly plush and relishable.

 Mt Difficulty Bannockburn Pinot Noir
2012 £25.99

No difficulty liking this new-oaked, full-frontal, ravishingly ripe Central Otago wine, but the price might prove a mountain to climb; 14% alcohol.

 F'Oz 2012 £10.69

Alentejo wine from indigenous grapes has dark, distinct, pungent slinky fruit; 14% alcohol.

 Waitrose Douro Valley Reserva
Quinta da Rosa 2011 £11.49

From the port vintage of the century (so far), a fine, sleekly oaked, minty and savoury table-wine variation on the fortified theme with a splendidly porty nose, if you get my drift.

RED WINES

S. AFRICA

8 **Southern Right Pinotage 2012**   £13.99
Distinctive peppery-tarry luxury-oaked Cape flagship wine for spicy dishes; 14% alcohol.

SPAIN

10 **Waitrose Mellow and Fruity Spanish Red 2013**   £4.99
Talk about doing what it says on the tin: this is a wonderfully mellow and fruity Campo de Borja pure Garnacha without fault, and an out-and-out bargain.

8 **Centellito del Sur Syrah Jumilla 2013**   £7.99
Jumilla's raspy reds are supposed to be from Monastrell grapes, but here's Syrah; it's packed with spicy-juicy fruit, not much like Jumilla, but much liked by me; 14% alcohol.

8 **Bodegas Sarria San Antonin Navarra Reserva 2004**   £9.99
Mature Merlot-Cabernet blend looks its age but sports a juicy-berry nose and has sinuous typical dark Navarra character in spite of Bordeaux cépage. A fascinating old wine that's still very much alive; 14% alcohol.

10 **Pablo the Cubist Old Vine Garnacha 2012**   £9.99
Picasso tribute wine from 'dusty, dry slate soils at an altitude of 1,000m' in Calatayud region is a perfect rendering of plummy, slinky black fruit contrived without oak and yet richly creamy in a transcendingly natural way; 14% alcohol. Simply amazing.

RED WINES

9 Pedra Viva Priorat 2013 £10.99

Young, unoaked, spicy but mellow and long-flavoured Garnacha-Carignan-Cabernet three-way split is remarkably rich and evolved, and very modestly priced for its much-vaunted region of origin; 14.5% alcohol.

9 Beronia Rioja Reserva 2009 £12.99

Naff label, but an outstanding Rioja with unusual density and tautness of fruit. You get a pleasing paradox of youthful vigour and plump, rounded maturity with controlled vanilla creaminess; 14% alcohol.

9 Torres Salmos Priorat 2011 £18.99

Intense cherry-prune-cassis silky Garnacha-based blend from Priorat's Porrera vineyards replanted by Torres (headquartered in neighbouring Catalan region Penedès) only a dozen years ago. This new and new-oaked vintage is already pure silk to drink now and should develop for years; 14.5% alcohol.

8 Luis Cañas Colección Privada Rioja Reserva 2006 £21.99

Esoteric, soupy, dark, thrillingly sleek, cassis-rich, mature 95% Tempranillo wine for special occasions; 14.5% alcohol.

9 Vega Sicilia Unico 2003 £215.00

Thank you, Waitrose, for letting me taste this spiffing Ribera del Duero wine. It enables the blurb writers to say that the prices of wines in this book range from under a fiver to £200-plus.

RED WINES

URUGUAY

8 Pizzorno Merlot/Tannat 2012   £8.79
Regional diversity is not the sole merit of this robust but carefully weighted brambly-fruit roast-beef-matcher.

PINK WINES

CHILE

8 Miguel Torres Las Mulas Cabernet Sauvignon Organic Rosé 2013   £8.99
Strong pink colour and matching intense strawberry-ripe summer-fruit flavour in this firm, dry, fresh and reassuring quality wine.

ENGLAND

7 Chapel Down English Rosé 2013   £10.99
Outrageous price but a pleasant dry soft-summer-fruit refresher for patriots; 10% alcohol.

FRANCE

8 La Grille Gamay Rosé 2013   £7.29
St Pourçain (Loire) light-magenta wine is eagerly crisp and fresh, finishing very dry.

8 Domaine Lafran-Veyrolles Bandol Rosé 2013   £14.99
From fashionable Bandol on the Riviera, the very pale copper colour is belied by the generous berry fruits and plump ripeness, trimmed up crisply dry with a tangy citrus acidity; serious rosé at a serious price.

GERMANY

7 Johann Wolf Pinot Noir Rosé 2013   £9.99
Pale-salmon colour, nice ripe raspberry whiff and a brisk finish to the sweetly ripe typical fruit; bit too expensive.

PINK WINES

GREECE

9 **Phaedra Xinomavro Rosé 2013** £8.99
Appropriately bright salmon-pink crunchy-fresh briar-fruit lemon-edged quality wine from Macedonian mountain region Florina.

ITALY

7 **Vignale Pinot Grigio Blush 2013** £6.29
I fear this will be popular; my detached report is that it's coral in colour, soft and yielding with a faint strawberry presence.

SPAIN

8 **Waitrose Ripe and Juicy Spanish Rosé 2013** £4.99
Soft Campo de Borja wine is pale magenta, just short of sweet, and forthcoming with brambly fruit.

WHITE WINES

AUSTRALIA

8 **Rolf Binder Highness Riesling 2013** £11.99
Limey and very full Eden Valley Riesling is in ideal balance; good Asian food match.

BRAZIL

8 **Waitrose Brazilian Chardonnay 2013** £8.99
Obviously one wishes the very best for Brazil's winemakers, and this sweet-apple unoaked natural-tasting dry wine does seem well-made.

ENGLAND

7 **Waitrose The Limes Selection Dry White 2013** £9.99
Bone-dry, Loire-style mainly Seyval Blanc contrivance from Dorking is fresh and lively, but expensive.

WHITE WINES

8 Champteloup Chardonnay 2013 £7.99

Not much Chardonnay in the Loire, but this one's legit: flinty-brisk, lots of crisp apple fruit, fresh and attention-grabbing.

8 Fief Guérin Muscadet Côtes de Grandlieu Sur Lie 2013 £7.99

Faint eggy smell did not deter me from trying this brisk but not sharp seaside-fresh moules-matcher in what has been reported as an impossibly difficult vintage.

10 La Grille Classic Sauvignon Blanc 2013 £8.79

This would pass convincingly for Sancerre, but is a humble generic Touraine wine, flinty-fresh, grassy-lush and sunny-ripe. In a harvest year I know has been very problematic in the Loire (and plenty of other places too), this is a little miracle.

8 Picpoul de Pinet Domaine de Félines-Jourdan 2013 £8.99

Tangy-fresh example of a trendy Mediterranean oyster wine has more fruit than most, from what has been a tricky vintage.

8 Château Tour Chapoux Sauvignon Blanc 2013 £9.99

Dry Bordeaux does include some Semillon and Muscadelle, and there is a little pineapple lushness alongside the tangy-fresh Sauvignon mainstream; nice one.

WHITE WINES

8 **Château de Montfort Vouvray Demi-Sec**
2013 **£11.99**
Ripe rather than semi-sweet Loire Chenin Blanc of
delightful hue and style; it's an aperitif wine, nicely
weighted with banana and honey in there somewhere,
and a fresh liveliness; 11% alcohol.

8 **Château de Fesles La Chapelle 2011** **£13.99**
Gold-coloured dry Chenin Blanc from Anjou has a
honeysuckle and brassica nose, lush, shrewdly oaked
tropical-fresh fruit, and sublime balance.

9 **Les Charmelles Pouilly-Fumé 2013** **£13.99**
Beguiling Loire Sauvignon classic really does have a
smoky pungency atop the lush ripe fruit and chalkstream
pure freshness; special-occasion wine.

8 **Waitrose Sancerre la Franchotte 2013** **£14.49**
Long-flavoured classic Sauvignon by esteemed Joseph
Mellot is deep-river fresh and jinglingly tangy.

8 **St Aubin 1er Cru Les Combes Domaine**
Gérard Thomas 2012 **£19.99**
Sumptuous white burgundy of revealing apple-pie purity
has a bright citrus acidity in ideal balance; nothing like a
slurp of the real thing from time to time.

8 **Grey Slate Dr L Private Reserve Riesling**
2013 **£9.99**
Spritz and sweet apple in this busily racy and delicate
Moselle; 10.5% alcohol.

WHITE WINES

GERMANY

🍷 8 **Leitz Rüdesheimer Rosengarten Riesling
Kabinett 2013** £14.49
Honeyed but bristlingly fresh and vivid Rheingau of fine balance; 10% alcohol.

GREECE

🍷 8 **Hatzidakis Assyrtiko 2013** £11.99
From the fashionable island of Santorini, an exotic fruit-salad, dry and stimulating holiday white; 14% alcohol.

ITALY

🍷 8 **Waitrose Pinot Grigio 2013** £6.49
Including 15% Chardonnay, a decent Trentino wine with a hint of almondy richness and lemon tang either side of the clean orchard fruit.

🍷 8 **Vernaccia di San Gimignano Teruzzi &
Puthod Rondolino 2013** £8.99
A wine of place – the tall-towered hilltown of San Gimignano is one of Tuscany's top tourist attractions – this has more than topographic appeal, having a good hit of white, leafy-herby, lime-edged fresh fruit.

🍷 8 **Zenato Villa Flora Lugana 2013** £9.49
Old Venetian friend on fine form has floral bloom, grassy zest and a discreet nutty richness; dry, fresh wine, reassuringly complete.

🍷 8 **La Monetta Gavi del Comune di Gavi 2013** £9.99
Unusually ascetic rendering of this currently voguish Piedmont dry white nevertheless has plenty of orchard-fruit charm.

WHITE WINES

7 Forrest Estate The Doctor's Sauvignon Blanc
2013 £8.99
Low-sugar experimental natural wine has grassy-nettly authenticity in spite of its reductive nature; 9.5% alcohol.

8 Waitrose in Partnership Sauvignon Blanc
2013 £10.49
Partner in Marlborough is Villa Maria; nettly fresh with a little extra sweet ripeness in the lush fruit.

8 Hunky Dory The Tangle 2013 £11.99
Miss the long-lost edelzwicker wines of Alsace? This Marlborough mélange is something akin, a plumply ripe, herbaceous blend of Pinot Gris, Gewürztraminer and Riesling with a nicely trim finish and 14% alcohol.

8 Waitrose Libra Verdejo Rueda 2013 £7.99
Seaside-fresh, uncomplicated, grassy-appley dry wine of distinct character.

8 Cune Barrel-Fermented Rioja 2013 £10.49
I reckon this is more austere than the creamy 2012 vintage, but it's still a rare example of white, oaked Rioja, and nicely made in the modern style (i.e. not yellow or oxidised, but fresh and perky).

9 Palacio de Fefiñanes Albariño 2013 £15.99
Exceptional Rias Baixas classic dry wine looks good in its snazzy package; you can smell the Atlantic breeze, roll in the seagrass and relish the lush white fruits.

SPARKLING WINES

9 Camel Valley Pinot Noir Brut 2010 £27.99
Impressively ripe and brightly polished champagne-style sparkler from Cornwall is an eye-opener into the genuinely prosperous future awaiting English fizz-makers (weather permitting).

**9 Cave de Lugny Blanc de Blancs
Crémant de Bourgogne** £13.49
Bready aromas, lush crisp-apple Chardonnay fruit, lovely lingering refreshment from Burgundy, whose marvellous crémant wines seem unfairly overlooked.

9 Waitrose Blanc de Noir Champagne Brut £21.99
Made exclusively from Pinot Noir, this creamy but zingy mature-tasting champagne lately pipped major brands in a much-reported consumer tasting. Judge for yourself.

—*Making the most of it*—

There has always been a lot of nonsense talked about the correct ways to serve wine. Red wine, we are told, should be opened and allowed to 'breathe' before pouring. White wine should be chilled. Wine doesn't go with soup, tomatoes or chocolate. You know the sort of thing.

It would all be simply laughable except that these daft conventions do make so many potential wine lovers nervous about the simple ritual of opening a bottle and sharing it around. Here is a short and opinionated guide to the received wisdom.

Breathing

Simply uncorking a wine for an hour or two before you serve it will make absolutely no difference to the way it tastes. However, if you wish to warm up an icy bottle of red by placing it near (never on) a radiator or fire, do remove the cork first. As the wine warms, even very slightly, it gives off gas, which will spoil the flavour if it cannot escape.

Chambré-ing

One of the more florid terms in the wine vocabulary. The idea is that red wine should be at the same temperature as the room (chambre) you're going to drink it in. In fairness, it makes sense – although the term harks back to the days when the only people who drank wine were those who could afford to keep it in the freezing cold vaulted cellars beneath their houses. The ridiculously high temperatures to which some homes are raised by central heating systems today are really far too warm for wine. But presumably those who live in such circumstances do so out of choice, and will prefer their wine to be similarly overheated.

Chilling

Drink your white wine as cold as you like. It's certainly true that good whites are at their best at a cool rather than at an icy temperature, but cheap and characterless wines can be improved immeasurably if they are cold enough – the anaesthetising effect of the temperature removes all sense of taste. Pay no attention to notions that red wine should not be served cool. There are plenty of lightweight reds that will respond very well to an hour in the fridge.

Corked wine

Wine trade surveys reveal that far too many bottles are in no fit state to be sold. The villain is very often cited as the cork. Cut from the bark of cork-oak trees cultivated for the purpose in Portugal and Spain, these natural stoppers have done sterling service for 200 years, but now face a crisis of confidence among wine producers. A diseased or damaged cork can make the wine taste stale because air has penetrated, or musty-mushroomy due to TCA, an infection of the raw material. These faults in wine, known as 'corked' or 'corky', should be immediately obvious, even in the humblest bottle, so you should return the bottle to the supplier and demand a refund.

Today, more and more wine producers are opting to close their bottles with polymer bungs. Some are designed to resemble the 'real thing' while others come in a rather disorienting range of colours – including black. While these things can be a pain to extract, there seems to be no evidence they do any harm to the wine. Don't 'lay down' bottles closed with polymer. The potential effects of years of contact with the plastic are yet to be scientifically established.

The same goes for screwcaps. These do have the merit of obviating the struggle with the corkscrew, but prolonged contact of the plastic liner with the wine might not be a good idea.

Corkscrews

The best kind of corkscrew is the 'waiter's friend' type. It looks like a pen-knife, unfolding a 'worm' (the helix or screw) and a lever device which, after the worm has been driven into the cork (try to centre it) rests on the lip of the bottle and enables you to withdraw the cork with minimal effort. Some have two-stage lips to facilitate the task. These devices are cheaper and longer-lasting than any of the more elaborate types, and are equally effective at withdrawing polymer bungs – which can be hellishly difficult to unwind from Teflon-coated 'continuous' corkscrews like the Screwpull.

Decanting

There are two views on the merits of decanting wines. The prevailing one seems to be that it is pointless and even pretentious. The other is that it can make real improvements in the way a wine tastes and is definitely worth the trouble.

Scientists, not usually much exercised by the finer nuances of wine, will tell you that exposure to the air causes wine to 'oxidise' – take in oxygen molecules that will quite quickly initiate the process of turning wine into vinegar – and anyone who has tasted a 'morning-after' glass of wine will no doubt vouch for this.

But the fact that wine does oxidise is a genuine clue to the reality of the effects of exposure to air. Shut inside its bottle, a young wine is very much a live substance, jumping with natural, but mysterious, compounds that can cause all sorts of strange taste sensations. But by exposing the wine to air these effects are markedly reduced.

In wines that spend longer in the bottle, the influence of these factors diminishes, in a process called 'reduction'. In red wines, the hardness of tannin – the natural preservative imparted into wine from the grape skins – gradually reduces, just as the raw purple colour darkens to ruby and later to orangey-brown.

I believe there is less reason for decanting old wines than new, unless the old wine has thrown a deposit and needs carefully to be poured off it. And in some light-bodied wines, such as older Rioja, decanting is probably a bad idea because it can accelerate oxidation all too quickly.

As to actual experiments, I have carried out several of my own, with wines opened in advance or wines decanted compared to the same wines just opened and poured, and my own unscientific judgement is that big, young, alcoholic reds can certainly be improved by aeration.

Washing glasses

If your wine glasses are of any value to you, don't put them in the dishwasher. Over time, they'll craze from the heat of the water. And they will not emerge in the glitteringly pristine condition suggested by the pictures on some detergent packets. For genuinely perfect glasses that will stay that way, wash them in hot soapy water, rinse with clean, hot water and dry immediately with a glass cloth kept exclusively for this purpose. Sounds like fanaticism, but if you take your wine seriously, you'll see there is sense in it.

Keeping wine

How long can you keep an opened bottle of wine before it goes downhill? Not long. A re-corked bottle with just a glassful out of it should stay fresh until the day after, but if there is a lot of air inside the bottle, the wine will oxidise, turning progressively stale and sour. Wine 'saving' devices that allow you to withdraw the air from the bottle via a punctured, self-sealing rubber stopper are variably effective, but don't expect these to keep a wine fresh for more than a couple of re-openings. A crafty method of keeping a half-finished bottle is to decant it, via a funnel, into a clean half bottle and recork.

Storing wine

Supermarket labels always seem to advise that 'this wine should be consumed within one year of purchase'. I think this is a wheeze to persuade customers to drink it up quickly and come back for more. Many of the more robust red wines are likely to stay in good condition for much more than one year, and plenty will actually improve with age. On the other hand, it is a sensible axiom that inexpensive dry white wines are better the younger they are. If you do intend to store wines for longer than a few weeks, do pay heed to the conventional wisdom that bottles are best stored in low, stable temperatures, preferably in the dark. Bottles closed with conventional corks should be laid on their side lest the corks dry out for lack of contact with the wine. But one of the notable advantages of the new closures now proliferating is that if your wine comes with a polymer 'cork' or a screwcap, you can safely store it upright.

Wine and food

Wine is made to be drunk with food, but some wines go better with particular dishes than others. It is no coincidence that Italian wines, characterised by soft, cherry fruit and a clean, mouth-drying finish, go so well with the sticky delights of pasta.

But it's personal taste rather than national associations that should determine the choice of wine with food. And if you prefer a black-hearted Argentinian Malbec to a brambly Italian Barbera with your Bolognese, that's fine.

The conventions that have grown up around wine and food pairings do make some sense, just the same. I was thrilled to learn in the early days of my drinking career that sweet, dessert wines can go well with strong blue cheese. As I don't much like puddings, but love sweet wines, I was eager to test this match – and I'm here to tell you that it works very well indeed as the end-piece to a grand meal in which there is cheese as well as pud on offer.

Red wine and cheese are supposed to be a natural match, but I'm not so sure. Reds can taste awfully tinny with soft cheeses such as Brie and Camembert, and even worse with goat's cheese. A really extravagant, yellow Australian Chardonnay will make a better match. Hard cheeses such as Cheddar and the wonderful Old Amsterdam (top-of-the-market Gouda) are better with reds.

And then there's the delicate issue of fish. Red wine is supposed to be a no-no. This might well be true of grilled and wholly unadorned white fish, such as sole or a delicate dish of prawns, scallops or crab. But what about oven-roasted monkfish or a substantial winter-season fish pie? An edgy red will do very well indeed, and provide much comfort for those many among us who simply prefer to drink red wine with food, and white wine on its own.

It is very often the method by which dishes are prepared, rather than their core ingredients, that determines which wine will work best. To be didactic, I would always choose Beaujolais or summer-fruit-style reds such as those from Pinot Noir grapes to go with a simple roast chicken. But if the bird is cooked as coq au vin with a hefty wine sauce, I would plump for a much more assertive red.

Some sauces, it is alleged, will overwhelm all wines. Salsa and curry come to mind. I have carried out a number of experiments into this great issue of our time, in my capacity as consultant to a company that specialises in supplying wines to Asian restaurants. One discovery I have made is that forcefully fruity dry white wines with keen acidity can go very well indeed even with fairly incendiary dishes. Sauvignon Blanc with Madras? Give it a try!

I'm also convinced, however, that some red wines will stand up very well to a bit of heat. The marvellously robust reds of Argentina made from Malbec grapes are good partners to Mexican chilli-hot recipes and salsa dishes. The dry, tannic edge to these wines provides a good counterpoint to the inflammatory spices in the food.

Some foods are supposedly impossible to match with wine. Eggs and chocolate are among the prime offenders. And yet, legendary cook Elizabeth David's best-selling autobiography was entitled *An Omelette and a Glass of Wine*, and the affiliation between chocolates and champagne is an unbreakable one. Taste is, after all, that most personally governed of all senses. If your choice is a boiled egg washed down with a glass of claret, who is to dictate otherwise?

What wine
——— words mean ———

Wine labels are getting crowded. It's mostly thanks to the unending torrent of new regulation. Lately, for example, the European Union has decided that all wines sold within its borders must display a health warning: 'Contains Sulphites'. All wines are made with the aid of preparations containing sulphur to combat diseases in the vineyards and bacterial infections in the winery. You can't make wine without sulphur. Even 'organic' wines are made with it. But some people are sensitive to the traces of sulphur in some wines, so we must all be informed of the presence of this hazardous material.

That's the way it is. And it might not be long before some even sterner warnings will be added about another ingredient in wine. Alcohol is the new tobacco, as the regulators see it, and in the near future we can look forward to some stern admonishments about the effects of alcohol. In the meantime, the mandatory information on every label includes the quantity, alcoholic strength and country of origin, along with the name of the producer. The region will be specified, vaguely on wines from loosely regulated countries such as Australia, and precisely on wines from over-regulated countries such as France. Wines from 'classic' regions of Europe – Bordeaux, Chianti, Rioja and so on – are mostly labelled according to their location rather than their constituent grape varieties. If it says Sancerre, it's taken as read that you either know it's made with Sauvignon Blanc grapes, or don't care.

Wines from just about everywhere else make no such assumptions. If a New Zealand wine is made from Sauvignon Blanc grapes, you can be sure the label will say so. This does quite neatly represent the gulf between the two worlds of winemaking. In traditional European regions, it's the place, the vineyard, that mostly determines the character of the wines. The French call it *terroir*, to encapsulate not just the lie of the land and the soil conditions but the wild variations in the weather from year to year as well. The grapes are merely the medium through which the timeless mysteries of the deep earth are translated into the ineffable glories of the wine, adjusted annually according to the vagaries of climate, variable moods of the winemaker, and who knows what else.

In the less arcane vineyards of the New World, the grape is definitely king. In hot valleys such as the Barossa (South Australia) or the Maipo (Chile), climate is relatively predictable and the soil conditions are managed by irrigation. It's the fruit that counts, and the style of the wine is determined by the variety – soft, spicy Shiraz; peachy, yellow Chardonnay and so on.

The main purpose of this glossary is, consequently, to give short descriptions of the 'classic' wines, including the names of the grapes they are made from, and of the 70-odd distinct grape varieties that make most of the world's wines. As well as these very brief descriptions, I have included equally shortened summaries of the regions and appellations of the better-known wines, along with some of the local terms used to indicate style and alleged qualities.

Finally, I have tried to explain in simple and rational terms the peculiar words I use in trying to convey the characteristics of wines described. 'Delicious' might need no further qualification, but the likes of 'bouncy', 'green' and 'liquorous' probably do.

A

abboccato – Medium-dry white wine style. Italy, especially Orvieto.

AC – *See* Appellation d'Origine Contrôlée.

acidity – To be any good, every wine must have the right level of acidity. It gives wine the element of dryness or sharpness it needs to prevent cloying sweetness or dull wateriness. If there is too much acidity, wine tastes raw or acetic (vinegary). Winemakers strive to create balanced acidity – either by cleverly controlling the natural processes, or by adding sugar and acid to correct imbalances.

aftertaste – The flavour that lingers in the mouth after swallowing the wine.

Aglianico – Black grape variety of southern Italy. It has romantic associations. When the ancient Greeks first colonised Italy in the seventh century BC, it was with the prime purpose of planting it as a vineyard (the Greek name for Italy was *Oenotria* – land of cultivated vines). The name for the vines the Greeks brought with them was Ellenico (as in Hellas, Greece), from which Aglianico is the modern rendering. To return to the point, these ancient vines, especially in the arid volcanic landscapes of Basilicata and Cilento, produce excellent dark, earthy and highly distinctive wines. A name to look out for.

Agriculture biologique – On French wine labels, an indication that the wine has been made by organic methods.

Albariño – White grape variety of Spain that makes intriguingly perfumed fresh and spicy dry wines, especially in esteemed Rias Baixas region.

alcohol – The alcohol levels in wines are expressed in terms of alcohol by volume ('abv'), that is, the percentage of the volume of the wine that is common, or ethyl, alcohol. A typical wine at 12 per cent abv is thus 12 parts alcohol and, in effect, 88 parts fruit juice.

The question of how much alcohol we can drink without harming ourselves in the short or long term is an impossible one to answer, but there is more or less general agreement among scientists that small amounts of alcohol are good for us, even if the only evidence of this is actuarial – the fact that mortality statistics show teetotallers live significantly shorter lives than moderate drinkers. According to the Department of Health, there are 'safe limits' to the amount of alcohol we should drink weekly. These limits are measured in units of alcohol, with a small glass of wine taken to be one unit. Men are advised that 28 units a week is the most they can drink without risk to health, and for women (whose liver function differs from that of men because of metabolic distinctions) the figure is 21 units.

If you wish to measure your consumption closely, note that a standard 75 cl bottle of wine at 12 per cent alcohol contains 9 units. A bottle of German Moselle at 8 per cent alcohol has only 6 units, but a bottle of Australian Chardonnay at 14 per cent has 10.5.

Alentejo – Wine region of southern Portugal (immediately north of the Algarve), with a fast-improving reputation, especially for sappy, keen reds from local grape varieties including Aragones, Castelão and Trincadeira.

Almansa – DO winemaking region of Spain inland from Alicante, making great-value red wines.

Alsace – France's easternmost wine-producing region lies between the Vosges Mountains and the River Rhine, with Germany beyond. These conditions make for the production of some of the world's most delicious and fascinating white wines, always sold under the name of their constituent grapes. Pinot Blanc is the most affordable – and is well worth looking out for. The 'noble' grape varieties of the region are Gewürztraminer, Muscat, Riesling and Pinot Gris and they are always made on a single-variety basis. The richest, most exotic wines are those from individual *grand cru* vineyards, which are named on the label. Some *vendange tardive* (late harvest) wines are made, but tend to be expensive. All the wines are sold in tall, slim green bottles known as flûtes that closely resemble those of the Mosel, and the names of producers and grape varieties are often German too, so it is widely assumed that Alsace wines are German in style, if not in nationality. But this is not the case in either particular. Alsace wines are dry and quite unique in character – and definitely French.

Amarone – Style of red wine made in Valpolicella, Italy. Specially selected grapes are held back from the harvest and stored for several months to dry them out. They are then pressed and fermented into a highly concentrated speciality dry wine. Amarone means 'bitter', describing the dry style of the flavour.

amontillado – *See* sherry.

aperitif – If a wine is thus described, I believe it will give more pleasure before a meal than with one. Crisp, low-alcohol German wines and other delicately flavoured whites (including many dry Italians) are examples.

Appellation d'Origine Contrôlée – Commonly abbreviated to AC or AOC, this is the system under which quality wines are defined in France. About a third of the country's vast annual output qualifies, and there are more than 400 distinct AC zones. The declaration of an AC on the label signifies that the wine meets standards concerning location of vineyards and wineries, grape varieties and limits on harvest per hectare, methods of cultivation and vinification, and alcohol content. Wines are inspected and tasted by state-appointed committees. The one major aspect of any given wine that an AC cannot guarantee is that you will like it – but it certainly improves the chances.

Appellation d'Origine Protégée (AOP) – Under recent EU rule changes, the AOC system is gradually transforming into AOP. In effect, it will mean little more than the exchange of 'controlled' with 'protected' on labels. One quirk of the new rules is that makers of AOP wines will be able to name the constituent grape variety or varieties on their labels, if they so wish.

Apulia – Anglicised name for Puglia.

Aragones – Synonym in Portugal, especially in the Alentejo region, for the Tempranillo grape variety of Spain.

Ardèche – Region of southern France to the west of the Rhône valley, home to a good vin de pays zone known as the Coteaux de L'Ardèche. Lots of decent-value reds from Syrah grapes, and some, less interesting, dry whites.

Arneis – White grape variety of Piedmont, north-west Italy. Makes dry whites with a certain almondy richness at often-inflated prices.

Assyrtiko – White grape variety of Greece now commonly named on dry white wines, sometimes of great quality, from the mainland and islands.

Asti – Town and major winemaking centre in Piedmont, Italy. The sparkling (spumante) sweet wines made from Moscato grapes are inexpensive and often delicious. Typical alcohol level is a modest 5 to 7 per cent.

attack – In wine tasting, the first impression made by the wine in the mouth.

Auslese – German wine-quality designation. *See* QmP.

B

Baga – Black grape variety indigenous to Portugal. Makes famously concentrated, juicy reds that get their deep colour from the grape's particularly thick skins. Look out for this name, now quite frequently quoted as the varietal on Portuguese wine labels. Often very good value for money.

balance – A big word in the vocabulary of wine tasting. Respectable wine must get two key things right: lots of fruitiness from the sweet grape juice, and plenty of acidity so the sweetness is 'balanced' with the crispness familiar in good dry whites and the dryness that marks out good reds. Some wines are noticeably 'well balanced' in that they have memorable fruitiness and the clean, satisfying 'finish' (last flavour in the mouth) that ideal acidity imparts.

Barbera – Black grape variety originally of Piedmont in Italy. Most commonly seen as Barbera d'Asti, the vigorously fruity red wine made around Asti – once better known for sweet sparkling Asti Spumante. Barbera grapes are now being grown in South America, often producing a sleeker, smoother style than at home in Italy.

Bardolino – Once fashionable, light red wine DOC of Veneto, north-west Italy. Bardolino is made principally from Corvina Veronese grapes plus Rondinella, Molinara and Negrara. Best wines are supposed to be those labelled Bardolino Superiore, a DOCG created in 2002. This classification closely specifies the permissible grape varieties and sets the alcohol level at a minimum of 12 per cent.

Barossa Valley – Famed vineyard region north of Adelaide, Australia, produces hearty reds principally from Shiraz, Cabernet Sauvignon and Grenache grapes, plus plenty of lush white wine from Chardonnay. Also known for limey, long-lived, mineral dry whites from Riesling grapes.

barrique – Barrel in French. *En barrique* on a wine label signifies the wine has been matured in oak.

Beaujolais – Unique red wines from the southern reaches of Burgundy, France, are made from Gamay grapes. Beaujolais nouveau, now deeply unfashionable, provides a friendly introduction to the bouncy, red-fruit style of the wine, but for the authentic experience, go for Beaujolais Villages, from the region's better, northern vineyards. There are ten AC zones within this northern sector making wines under their own names. Known as the *crus*, these are Brouilly, Chénas, Chiroubles, Côte de Brouilly, Fleurie, Juliénas, Morgon, Moulin à Vent, Regnié and St Amour and produce most of the best wines of the region. Prices are higher than those for Beaujolais Villages, but by no means always justifiably so.

Beaumes de Venise – Village near Châteauneuf du Pape in France's Rhône valley, famous for sweet and alcoholic wine from Muscat grapes. Delicious, grapey wines. A small number of growers also make strong (sometimes rather tough) red wines under the village name.

Beaune – One of the two winemaking centres (the other is Nuits St Georges) at the heart of Burgundy in France. Three of the region's humbler appellations take the name of the town: Côtes de Beaune, Côtes de Beaune Villages and Hautes Côtes de Beaune. Wines made under these ACs are often, but by no means always, good value for money.

berry fruit – Some red wines deliver a burst of flavour in the mouth that corresponds to biting into a newly picked berry – strawberry, blackberry, etc. So a wine described as having berry fruit (by this writer, anyway) has freshness, liveliness and immediate appeal.

bianco – White wine, Italy.

Bical – White grape variety principally of Dão region of northern Portugal. Not usually identified on labels, because most of it goes into inexpensive sparkling wines. Can make still wines of very refreshing crispness.

biodynamics – A cultivation method taking the organic approach several steps further. Biodynamic winemakers plant and tend their vineyards according to a date and time calendar 'in harmony' with the movements of the planets. Some of France's best-known wine estates subscribe, and many more are going that way. It might all sound bonkers, but it's salutary to learn that biodynamics is based on principles first described by a very eminent man, the Austrian educationist Rudolf Steiner. He's lately been in the news for having written, in 1919, that farmers crazy enough to feed animal products to cattle would drive the livestock 'mad'.

bite – In wine tasting, the impression on the palate of a wine with plenty of acidity and, often, tannin.

blanc – White wine, France.

blanc de blancs – White wine from white grapes, France. May seem to be stating the obvious, but some white wines (e.g. champagne) are made, partially or entirely, from black grapes.

blanc de noirs – White wine from black grapes, France. Usually sparkling (especially champagne) made from black Pinot Meunier and Pinot Noir grapes, with no Chardonnay or other white varieties.

blanco – White wine, Spain and Portugal.

Blauer Zweigelt – Black grape variety of Austria, making a large proportion of the country's red wines, some of excellent quality.

Bobal – Black grape variety mostly of south-eastern Spain. Thick skin is good for colour and juice contributes acidity to blends.

bodega – In Spain, a wine producer or wine shop.

Bonarda – Black grape variety of northern Italy. Now more widely planted in Argentina, where it makes rather elegant red wines, often representing great value.

botrytis – Full name, *botrytis cinerea*, is that of a beneficent fungus that can attack ripe grape bunches late in the season, shrivelling the berries to a gruesome-looking mess, which yields concentrated juice of prized sweetness. Cheerfully known as 'noble rot', this fungus is actively encouraged by winemakers in regions as diverse as Sauternes (in Bordeaux), Monbazillac (in Bergerac), the Rhine and Mosel valleys, Hungary's Tokaji region and South Australia to make ambrosial dessert wines.

bouncy – The feel in the mouth of a red wine with young, juicy fruitiness. Good Beaujolais is bouncy, as are many north-west-Italian wines from Barbera and Dolcetto grapes.

Bourgogne Grand Ordinaire – Former AC of Burgundy, France. *See* Coteaux Bourguignons.

Bourgueil – Appellation of Loire Valley, France. Long-lived red wines from Cabernet Franc grapes.

briary – In wine tasting, associated with the flavours of fruit from prickly bushes such as blackberries.

brûlé – Pleasant burnt-toffee taste or smell, as in crème brûlée.

brut – Driest style of sparkling wine. Originally French, for very dry champagnes specially developed for the British market, but now used for sparkling wines from all round the world.

Buzet – Little-seen AC of south-west France overshadowed by Bordeaux but producing some characterful ripe reds.

C

Cabardès – AC for red and rosé wines from area north of Carcassonne, Aude, France. Principally Cabernet Sauvignon and Merlot grapes.

Cabernet Franc – Black grape variety originally of France. It makes the light-bodied and keenly edged red wines of the Loire Valley – such as Chinon and Saumur. And it is much grown in Bordeaux, especially in the appellation of St Emilion. Also now planted in Argentina, Australia and North America. Wines, especially in the Loire, are characterised by a leafy, sappy style and bold fruitiness. Most are best enjoyed young.

Cabernet Sauvignon – Black (or, rather, blue) grape variety now grown in virtually every wine-producing nation. When perfectly ripened, the grapes are smaller than many other varieties and have particularly thick skins. This means that when pressed, Cabernet grapes have a high proportion of skin to juice – and that makes for wine with lots of colour and tannin. In Bordeaux, the grape's traditional home, the grandest Cabernet-based wines have always been known as *vins de garde* (wines to keep) because they take years, even decades, to evolve as the effect of all that skin extraction preserves the fruit all the way to magnificent maturity. But in today's impatient world, these grapes are exploited in modern winemaking techniques to produce the sublime flavours of mature Cabernet without having to hang around for lengthy periods awaiting maturation. While there's nothing like a fine, ten-year-old claret (and nothing quite as expensive), there are many excellent Cabernets from around the world that amply illustrate this grape's characteristics. Classic smells and flavours include blackcurrants, cedar wood, chocolate, tobacco – even violets.

Cahors – An AC of the Lot Valley in south-west France once famous for 'black wine'. This was a curious concoction of straightforward wine mixed with a soupy must, made by boiling up new-pressed juice to concentrate it (through evaporation) before fermentation. The myth is still perpetuated that Cahors wine continues to be made in this way, but production on this basis actually ceased 150 years ago. Cahors today is no stronger, or blacker, than the wines of neighbouring appellations.

Cairanne – Village of the appellation collectively known as the Côtes du Rhône in southern France. Cairanne is one of several villages entitled to put their name on the labels of wines made within their AC boundary, and the appearance of this name is quite reliably an indicator of a very good wine indeed.

Calatayud – DO (quality wine zone) near Zaragoza in the Aragon region of northern Spain where they're making some astonishingly good wines at bargain prices, mainly reds from Garnacha and Tempranillo grapes. These are the varieties that go into the light and oaky wines of Rioja, but in Calatayud, the wines are dark, dense and decidedly different.

Cannonau – Black grape native to Sardinia by name, but in fact the same variety as the ubiquitous Grenache of France (and Garnacha of Spain).

cantina sociale – *See* co-op.

Carignan – Black grape variety of Mediterranean France. It is rarely identified on labels, but is a major constituent of wines from the southern Rhône and Languedoc-Roussillon regions. Known as Carignano in Italy and Cariñena in Spain.

Cariñena – A region of north-east Spain, south of Navarra, known for substantial reds, as well as the Spanish name for the Carignan grape (*qv*).

Carmenère – Black grape variety once widely grown in Bordeaux but abandoned due to cultivation problems. Lately revived in South America where it is producing fine wines, sometimes with echoes of Bordeaux.

cassis – As a tasting note, signifies a wine that has a noticeable blackcurrant-concentrate flavour or smell. Much associated with the Cabernet Sauvignon grape.

Castelao – Portuguese black grape variety. Same as Periquita.

Catarratto – White grape variety of Sicily. In skilled hands it can make anything from keen, green-fruit dry whites to lush, oaked super-ripe styles. Also used for Marsala.

cat's pee – In tasting notes, a mildly jocular reference to a certain style of Sauvignon Blanc wine.

cava – The sparkling wine of Spain. Most originates in Catalonia, but the Denominación de Origen (DO) guarantee of authenticity is open to producers in many regions of the country. Much cava is very reasonably priced even though it is made by the same method as champagne – second fermentation in bottle, known in Spain as the *método clásico*.

CdR – Côtes du Rhône.

Cépage – Grape variety, French. 'Cépage Merlot' on a label simply means the wine is made largely or exclusively from Merlot grapes.

Chablis – Northernmost AC of France's Burgundy region. Its dry white wines from Chardonnay grapes are known for their fresh and steely style, but the best wines also age very gracefully into complex classics.

Chambourcin – Sounds like a cream cheese but it's a relatively modern (1963) French hybrid black grape that makes some good non-appellation lightweight-but-concentrated reds in the Loire Valley and now some heftier versions in Australia.

Chardonnay – The world's most popular grape variety. Said to originate from the village of Chardonnay in the Mâconnais region of southern Burgundy, the vine is now planted in every wine-producing nation. Wines are commonly characterised by generous colour and sweet-apple smell, but styles range from lean and sharp to opulently rich. Australia started the craze for oaked Chardonnay, the gold-coloured, super-ripe, buttery 'upfront' wines that are a caricature of lavish and outrageously expensive burgundies such as Meursault and Puligny-Montrachet. Rich to the point of egginess, these Aussie pretenders are now giving way to a sleeker, more minerally style with much less oak presence – if any at all. California and Chile, New Zealand and South Africa are competing hard to imitate the Burgundian style, and Australia's success in doing so.

Châteauneuf du Pape – Famed appellation centred on a picturesque village of the southern Rhône valley in France where in the 1320s French Pope Clement V had a splendid new château built for himself as a country retreat amidst his vineyards. The red wines of the AC, which can be made from 13 different grape varieties but principally Grenache, Syrah and Mourvèdre, are regarded as the best of the southern Rhône and have become rather expensive – but they can be sensationally good. Expensive white wines are also made.

Chenin Blanc – White grape variety of the Loire Valley, France. Now also grown farther afield, especially in South Africa. Makes dry, soft white wines and also rich, sweet styles. Sadly, many low-cost Chenin wines are bland and uninteresting.

cherry – In wine tasting, either a pale red colour or, more commonly, a smell or flavour akin to the sun-warmed, bursting sweet ripeness of cherries. Many Italian wines, from lightweights such as Bardolino and Valpolicella to serious Chianti, have this character. 'Black cherry' as a description is often used of Merlot wines – meaning they are sweet but have a firmness associated with the thicker skins of black cherries.

Cinsault – Black grape variety of southern France, where it is invariably blended with others in wines of all qualities ranging from vin de pays to the pricy reds of Châteauneuf du Pape. Also much planted in South Africa. The effect in wine is to add keen aromas (sometimes compared with turpentine!) and softness to the blend. The name is often spelt Cinsaut.

Clape, La – A small *cru* (defined quality-vineyard area) within the Coteaux du Languedoc where the growers make some seriously delicious red wines, mainly from Carignan, Grenache and Syrah grapes. A name worth looking out for on labels from the region.

claret – The red wine of Bordeaux, France. It comes from Latin *clarus*, meaning 'clear', recalling a time when the red wines of the region were much lighter in colour than they are now.

clarete – On Spanish labels indicates a pale-coloured red wine. Tinto signifies a deeper hue.

classed growth – English translation of French *cru classé* describes a group of 60 individual wine estates in the Médoc district of Bordeaux, which in 1855 were granted this new status on the basis that their wines were the most expensive at that time. The classification was a promotional wheeze to attract attention to the Bordeaux stand at that year's Great Exhibition in Paris. Amazingly, all of the 60 wines concerned are still in production and most still occupy more or less their original places in the pecking order price-wise. The league was divided up into five divisions from *Premier Grand Cru Classé* (just four wines originally, with one promoted in 1971 – the only change ever made to the classification) to *Cinquième Grand Cru Classé*. Other regions of Bordeaux, notably Graves and St Emilion, have since imitated Médoc and introduced their own rankings of *cru classé* estates.

classic – An overused term in every respect – wine descriptions being no exception. In this book, the word is used to describe a very good wine of its type. So, a 'classic' Cabernet Sauvignon is one that is recognisably and admirably characteristic of that grape.

Classico – Under Italy's wine laws, this word appended to the name of a DOC zone has an important significance. The classico wines of the region can only be made from vineyards lying in the best-rated areas, and wines thus labelled (e.g. Chianti Classico, Soave Classico, Valpolicella Classico) can be reliably counted on to be a cut above the rest.

Colombard – White grape variety of southern France. Once employed almost entirely for making the wine that is distilled for armagnac and cognac brandies, but lately restored to varietal prominence in the Vin de Pays des Côtes de Gascogne where high-tech wineries turn it into a fresh and crisp, if unchallenging, dry wine at a budget price. But beware, cheap Colombard (especially from South Africa) can still be very dull.

Conca de Barbera – Winemaking region of Catalonia, Spain.

co-op – Very many of France's good-quality, inexpensive wines are made by co-operatives. These are wine-producing factories whose members, and joint-owners, are local *vignerons* (vine growers). Each year they sell their harvests to the co-op for turning into branded wines. In Italy, co-op wines can be identified by the words *Cantina Sociale* on the label and in Germany by the term *Winzergenossenschaft*.

Corbières – A name to look out for. It's an AC of France's Midi (deep south) and produces countless robust reds and a few interesting whites, often at bargain prices.

Cortese – White grape variety of Piedmont, Italy. At its best, makes amazingly delicious, keenly brisk and fascinating wines, including those of the Gavi DOCG. Worth seeking out.

Costières de Nîmes – Until 1989, this AC of southern France was known as the Costières de Gard. It forms a buffer between the southern Rhône and Languedoc-Roussillon regions, and makes wines from broadly the same range of grape varieties. It's a name to look out for, the best red wines being notable for their concentration of colour and fruit, with the earthy-spiciness of the better Rhône wines and a likeable liquorice note. A few good white wines, too, and even a decent rosé or two.

Côte – In French, it simply means a side, or slope, of a hill. The implication in wine terms is that the grapes come from a vineyard ideally situated for maximum sunlight, good drainage and the unique soil conditions prevailing on the hill in question. It's fair enough to claim that vines grown on slopes might get more sunlight than those grown on the flat, but there is no guarantee whatsoever that any wine labelled 'Côtes du' this or that is made from grapes grown on a hillside anyway. Côtes du Rhône wines are a case in point. Many 'Côtes' wines come from entirely level vineyards and it is worth remembering that many of the vineyards of Bordeaux, producing most of the world's priciest wines, are little short of prairie-flat. The quality factor is determined much more significantly by the weather and the talents of the winemaker.

Coteaux Bourguignons – Generic AC of Burgundy, France, since 2011 for red and rosé wines from Pinot Noir and Gamay grapes, and white wines from (principally) Chardonnay and Bourgogne Aligoté grapes. The AC replaces the former appellation Bourgogne Grand Ordinaire.

Côtes de Blaye – Appellation Contrôlée zone of Bordeaux on the right bank of the River Gironde, opposite the more prestigious Médoc zone of the left bank. Best-rated vineyards qualify for the AC Premières Côtes de Blaye. A couple of centuries ago, Blaye (pronounced 'bligh') was the grander of the two, and even today makes some wines that compete well for quality, and at a fraction of the price of wines from its more fashionable rival across the water.

Côtes de Bourg – AC neighbouring Côtes de Blaye, making red wines of fast-improving quality and value.

Côtes du Luberon – Appellation Contrôlée zone of Provence in south-east France. Wines, mostly red, are similar in style to Côtes du Rhône.

Côtes du Rhône – One of the biggest and best-known appellations of south-east France, covering an area roughly defined by the southern reaches of the valley of the River Rhône. Long notorious for cheap and execrable reds, the Côtes du Rhône AC has lately achieved remarkable improvements in quality at all points along the price scale. Lots of brilliant-value warm and spicy reds, principally from Grenache and Syrah grapes. There are also some white and rosé wines.

Côtes du Rhône Villages – Appellation within the larger Côtes du Rhône AC for wine of supposed superiority made in a number of zones associated with a long list of nominated individual villages.

Côtes du Roussillon – Huge appellation of south-west France known for strong, dark, peppery reds often offering very decent value.

Côtes du Roussillon Villages – Appellation for superior wines from a number of nominated locations within the larger Roussillon AC. Some of these village wines can be of exceptional quality and value.

crianza – Means 'nursery' in Spanish. On Rioja and Navarra wines, the designation signifies a wine that has been nursed through a maturing period of at least a year in oak casks and a further six months in bottle before being released for sale.

cru – A word that crops up with confusing regularity on French wine labels. It means 'the growing' or 'the making' of a wine and asserts that the wine concerned is from a specific vineyard. Under the Appellation Contrôlée rules, countless *crus* are classified in various hierarchical ranks. Hundreds of individual vineyards are described as *premier cru* or *grand cru* in the classic wine regions of Alsace, Bordeaux, Burgundy and Champagne. The common denominator is that the wine can be counted on to be enormously expensive. On humbler wines, the use of the word *cru* tends to be mere decoration.

cru classé – *See* classed growth.

cuve – A vat for wine. French.

cuvée – French for the wine in a *cuve*, or vat. The word is much used on labels to imply that the wine is from just one vat, and thus of unique, unblended character. *Première cuvée* is supposedly the best wine from a given pressing because the grapes have had only the initial, gentle squashing to extract the free-run juice. Subsequent *cuvées* will have been from harsher pressings, grinding the grape pulp to extract the last drop of juice.

D

Dão – Major wine-producing region of northern Portugal now turning out much more interesting reds than it used to – worth looking out for anything made by mega-producer Sogrape.

demi sec – 'Half-dry' style of French (and some other) wines. Beware. It can mean anything from off-dry to cloyingly sweet.

DO – Denominación de Origen, Spain's wine-regulating scheme, similar to France's AC, but older – the first DO region was Rioja, from 1926. DO wines are Spain's best, accounting for a third of the nation's annual production.

DOC – Stands for Denominazione di Origine Controllata, Italy's equivalent of France's AC. The wines are made according to the stipulations of each of the system's 300-plus denominated zones of origin, along with a further 73 zones, which enjoy the superior classification of DOCG (DOC with *e Garantita* – guaranteed – appended).

Durif – Rare black grape variety mostly of California, where it is also known as Petite Sirah, but with some plantings in Australia.

E

earthy – A tricky word in the wine vocabulary. In this book, its use is meant to be complimentary. It indicates that the wine somehow suggests the soil the grapes were grown in, even (perhaps a shade too poetically) the landscape in which the vineyards lie. The amazing-value red wines of the torrid, volcanic southernmost regions of Italy are often described as earthy. This is an association with the pleasantly 'scorched' back-flavour in wines made from the ultra-ripe harvests of this near-sub-tropical part of the world.

edge – A wine with edge is one with evident (although not excessive) acidity.

élevé – 'Brought up' in French. Much used on wine labels where the wine has been matured (brought up) in oak barrels, *élevé en fûts de chêne*, to give it extra dimensions.

Entre Deux Mers – Meaning 'between two seas', it's a region lying between the Dordogne and Garonne rivers of Bordeaux, now mainly known for dry white wines from Sauvignon and Semillon grapes.

Estremadura – Wine-producing region occupying Portugal's coastal area north of Lisbon. Lots of interesting wines from indigenous grape varieties, usually at bargain prices. If a label mentions Estremadura, it is a safe rule that there might be something good within.

Extremadura – Minor wine-producing region of western Spain abutting the frontier with Portugal's Alentejo region. Not to be confused with Estremadura of Portugal (above).

F

Falanghina – Revived ancient grape variety of southern Italy now making some superbly fresh and tangy white wines.

Faugères – AC of the Languedoc in south-west France. Source of many hearty, economic reds.

Feteasca – White grape variety widely grown in Romania. Name means 'maiden's grape' and the wine tends to be soft and slightly sweet.

Fiano – White grape variety of the Campania of southern Italy and Sicily, lately revived. It is said to have been cultivated by the ancient Romans for a wine called Apianum.

finish – The last flavour lingering in the mouth after wine has been swallowed.

fino – Pale and very dry style of sherry. You drink it thoroughly chilled – and you don't keep it any longer after opening than other dry white wines. Needs to be fresh to be at its best.

Fitou – One of the first 'designer' wines, it's an appellation in France's Languedoc region, where production is dominated by one huge co-operative, the Vignerons de Mont Tauch. Back in the 1970s, this co-op paid a corporate-image company to come up with a Fitou logo and label-design style, and the wines have prospered ever since. And it's not just packaging – Fitou at all price levels can be very good value, especially from the Mont Tauch co-op.

flabby – Fun word describing a wine that tastes dilute or watery, with insufficient acidity.

Frappato – Black grape variety of Sicily. Light red wines.

fruit – In tasting terms, the fruit is the greater part of the overall flavour of a wine. The wine is (or should be) after all, composed entirely of fruit.

G

Gamay – The black grape that makes all red Beaujolais and some ordinary burgundy. It is a pretty safe rule to avoid Gamay wines from any other region, but there are exceptions.

Garganega – White grape variety of the Veneto region of north-east Italy. Best known as the principal ingredient of Soave, but occasionally included in varietal blends and mentioned as such on labels. Correctly pronounced 'gar-GAN-iga'.

Garnacha – Spanish black grape variety synonymous with Grenache of France. It is blended with Tempranillo to make the red wines of Rioja and Navarra, and is now quite widely cultivated elsewhere in Spain to make grippingly fruity varietals.

garrigue – Arid land of France's deep south giving its name to a style of red wine that notionally evokes the herby, heated, peppery flavours associated with such a landscape. A tricky metaphor!

Gavi – DOCG for dry but rich white wine from Cortese grapes in Piedmont, north-west Italy. Trendy Gavi di Gavi wines tend to be enjoyably lush, but are rather expensive.

Gewürztraminer – One of the great grape varieties of Alsace, France. At their best, the wines are perfumed with lychees and are richly, spicily fruity, yet quite dry. Gewürztraminer from Alsace can be expensive, but the grape is also grown with some success in Germany, Italy, New Zealand and South America, at more approachable prices. Pronounced 'ge-VOORTS-traminner'.

Givry – AC for red and white wines in the Côte Chalonnaise sub-region of Burgundy. Source of some wonderfully natural-tasting reds that might be lighter than those of the more prestigious Côte d'Or to the north, but have great merits of their own. Relatively, the wines are often underpriced.

Glera – Alternative name for Prosecco grape of northern Italy.

Godello – White grape variety of Galicia, Spain.

Graciano – Black grape variety of Spain that is one of the minor constituents of Rioja. Better known in its own right in Australia where it can make dense, spicy, long-lived red wines.

green – I don't often use this in the pejorative. Green, to me, is a likeable degree of freshness, especially in Sauvignon Blanc wines.

Grecanico – White grape variety of southern Italy, especially Sicily. Aromatic, grassy dry white wines.

Greco – White grape variety of southern Italy believed to be of ancient Greek origin. Big-flavoured dry white wines.

Grenache – The mainstay of the wines of the southern Rhône Valley in France. Grenache is usually the greater part of the mix in Côtes du Rhône reds and is widely planted right across the neighbouring Languedoc-Roussillon region. It's a big-cropping variety that thrives even in the hottest climates and is really a blending grape – most commonly with Syrah, the noble variety of the northern Rhône. Few French wines are labelled with its name, but the grape has caught on in Australia in a big way and it is now becoming a familiar varietal, known for strong, dark liquorous reds. Grenache is the French name for what is originally a Spanish variety, Garnacha.

Grillo – White grape of Sicily said to be among the island's oldest indigenous varieties, pre-dating the arrival of the Greeks in 600 BC. Much used for fortified Marsala, it has lately been revived for interesting, aromatic dry table wines.

grip – In wine-tasting terminology, the sensation in the mouth produced by a wine that has a healthy quantity of tannin in it. A wine with grip is a good wine. A wine with too much tannin, or which is still too young (the tannin hasn't 'softened' with age) is not described as having grip, but as mouth-puckering – or simply undrinkable.

Grolleau – Black grape variety of the Loire Valley principally cultivated for Rosé d'Anjou.

Gros Plant – White grape variety of the Pays Nantais in France's Loire estuary; synonymous with the Folle Blanche grape of south-west France.

Grüner Veltliner – The 'national' white-wine grape of Austria. In the past it made mostly soft, German-style everyday wines, but now is behind some excellent dry styles, too.

H

halbtrocken – 'Half-dry' in Germany's wine vocabulary. A reassurance that the wine is not some ghastly sugared Liebfraumilch-style confection.

hard – In red wine, a flavour denoting excess tannin, probably due to immaturity.

Haut-Médoc – Extensive AOC of Bordeaux accounting for the greater part of the vineyard area to the north of the city of Bordeaux and west of the Gironde river. The Haut-Médoc incorporates the prestigious commune-AOCs of Listrac, Margaux, Moulis, Pauillac, St Estephe and St Julien.

hock – The wine of Germany's Rhine river valleys. Traditionally, but no longer consistently, it comes in brown bottles, as distinct from the wine of the Mosel river valleys – which comes in green ones.

I

Indication Géographique Protégée (IGP) – Introduced to France in 2010 under new EU-wide wine-designation rules, IGP covers the wines hitherto known as vins de pays. Some wines are already being labelled IGP, but established vins de pays producers are unlikely to redesignate their products in a hurry, and are not obliged to do so. Some will abbreviate, so, for example, Vin de Pays d'Oc shortens to Pays d'Oc.

Indicazione Geografica Tipica – Italian wine-quality designation, broadly equivalent to France's vin de pays. The label has to state the geographical location of the vineyard and will often (but not always) state the principal grape varieties from which the wine is made.

isinglass – A gelatinous material used in fining (clarifying) wine. It is derived from fish bladders and consequently is eschewed by makers of 'vegetarian' wines.

J

jammy – The 'sweetness' in dry red wines is supposed to evoke ripeness rather than sugariness. Sometimes, flavours include a sweetness reminiscent of jam. Usually a fault in the winemaking technique.

Jerez – Wine town of Andalucia, Spain, and home to sherry. The English word 'sherry' is a simple mispronunciation of Jerez.

joven – Young wine, Spanish. In regions such as Rioja, *vino joven* is a synonym for *sin crianza*, which means 'without ageing' in cask or bottle.

Jura – Wine region of eastern France incorporating four AOCs, Arbois, Château-Chalon, Côtes du Jura and L'Etoile. Known for still red, white and rosé wines and sparkling wines as well as exotic *vin de paille* and *vin jaune*.

Jurançon – Appellation for white wines from Courbu and Manseng grapes at Pau, south-west France.

K

Kabinett – Under Germany's bewildering wine-quality rules, this is a classification of a top-quality (QmP) wine. Expect a keen, dry, racy style. The name comes from the cabinet or cupboard in which winemakers traditionally kept their most treasured bottles.

Kekfrankos – Black grape variety of Hungary, particularly the Sopron region, which makes some of the country's more interesting red wines, characterised by colour and spiciness. Same variety as Austria's Blaufrankisch.

L

Ladoix – Unfashionable AC at northern edge of Côtes de Beaune makes some of Burgundy's true bargain reds. A name to look out for.

Lambrusco – The name is that of a black grape variety widely grown across northern Italy. True Lambrusco wine is red, dry and very slightly sparkling, but from the 1980s Britain was deluged with a strange, sweet manifestation of the style, which has done little to enhance the good name of the original. Good Lambrusco is delicious and fun, but in this country now very hard to find.

Languedoc-Roussillon – Vast area of southern France, including the country's south-west Mediterranean region. The source, now, of many great-value wines from countless ACs and vin de pays zones.

lees – The detritus of the winemaking process that collects in the bottom of the vat or cask. Wines left for extended periods on the lees can acquire extra dimensions of flavour, in particular a 'leesy' creaminess.

legs – The liquid residue left clinging to the sides of the glass after wine has been swirled. The persistence of the legs is an indicator of the weight of alcohol. Also known as 'tears'.

lieu dit – This is starting to appear on French wine labels. It translates as an 'agreed place' and is an area of vineyard defined as of particular character or merit, but not classified under wine law. Usually, the *lieu dit*'s name is stated, with the implication that the wine in question has special value.

liquorice – The pungent, slightly burnt flavours of this once-fashionable confection are detectable in some wines made from very ripe grapes, for example, the Malbec harvested in Argentina and several varieties grown in the very hot vineyards of southernmost Italy. A close synonym is 'tarry'. This characteristic is by no means a fault in red wine, unless very dominant, but it can make for a challenging flavour that might not appeal to all tastes.

liquorous – Wines of great weight and glyceriney texture (evidenced by the 'legs', or 'tears', which cling to the glass after the wine has been swirled) are always noteworthy. The connection with liquor is drawn in respect of the feel of the wine in the mouth, rather than with the higher alcoholic strength of spirits.

Lirac – Village and AOC of southern Rhône Valley, France. A near-neighbour of the esteemed appellation of Châteauneuf du Pape, Lirac makes red wine of comparable depth and complexity, at competitive prices.

Lugana – DOC of Lombardy, Italy, known for a dry white wine that is often of real distinction – rich, almondy stuff from the ubiquitous Trebbiano grape.

M

Macabeo – One of the main grapes used for cava, the sparkling wine of Spain. It is the same grape as Viura.

Mâcon – Town and collective appellation of southern Burgundy, France. Lightweight white wines from Chardonnay grapes and similarly light reds from Pinot Noir and some Gamay. The better ones, and the ones exported, have the AC Mâcon-Villages and there are individual village wines with their own ACs including Mâcon-Clessé, Mâcon-Viré and Mâcon-Lugny.

Malbec – Black grape variety grown on a small scale in Bordeaux, and the mainstay of the wines of Cahors in France's Dordogne region under the name Cot. Now much better known for producing big butch reds in Argentina.

manzanilla – Pale, very dry sherry of Sanlucar de Barrameda, a resort town on the Bay of Cadiz in Spain. Manzanilla is proud to be distinct from the pale, very dry fino sherry of the main producing town of Jerez de la Frontera an hour's drive inland. Drink it chilled and fresh – it goes downhill in an opened bottle after just a few days, even if kept (as it should be) in the fridge.

Margaret River – Vineyard region of Western Australia regarded as ideal for grape varieties including Cabernet Sauvignon. It has a relatively cool climate and a reputation for making sophisticated wines, both red and white.

Marlborough – Best-known vineyard region of New Zealand's South Island has a cool climate and a name for brisk but cerebral Sauvignon Blanc and Chardonnay wines.

Marsanne – White grape variety of the northern Rhône Valley and, increasingly, of the wider south of France. It's known for making well-coloured wines with heady aroma and fruit.

Mataro – Black grape variety of Australia. It's the same as the Mourvèdre of France and Monastrell of Spain.

Mazuelo – Spanish name for France's black grape variety Carignan.

McLaren Vale – Vineyard region south of Adelaide in south-east Australia. Known for blockbuster Shiraz (and Chardonnay) that can be of great balance and quality from winemakers who keep the ripeness under control.

meaty – Weighty, rich red wine style.

Mencia – Black grape variety of Galicia and north-west Spain. Light red wines.

Mendoza – The region to watch in Argentina. Lying to the east of the Andes mountains, just about opposite the best vineyards of Chile on the other side, Mendoza accounts for the bulk of Argentine wine production, with quality improving fast.

Merlot – One of the great black wine grapes of Bordeaux, and now grown all over the world. The name is said to derive from the French *merle*, meaning a blackbird. Characteristics of Merlot-based wines attract descriptions such as 'plummy' and 'plump' with black-cherry aroma. The grapes are larger than most, and thus have less skin in proportion to their flesh. This means the resulting wines have less tannin than wines from smaller-berry varieties such as Cabernet Sauvignon, and are therefore, in the Bordeaux context at least, more suitable for drinking while still relatively young.

middle palate – In wine tasting, the impression given by the wine when it is held in the mouth.

Midi – Catch-all term for the deep south of France west of the Rhône Valley.

mineral – I am trying to excise this overused word from my notes, but not so far managing to do so with much conviction. To me it evokes flavours such as the stone-pure freshness of some Loire dry whites, or the steely quality of the more austere style of the Chardonnay grape, especially in Chablis. Mineral really just means something mined, as in dug out of the ground, like iron ore (as in steel) or rock, as in, er, stone. Maybe there's something in it, but I am not entirely confident.

Minervois – AC for (mostly) red wines from vineyards around the town of Minerve in the Languedoc-Roussillon region of France. Often good value. The new Minervois La Livinière AC – a sort of Minervois *grand cru* – is host to some great estates including Château Maris and Vignobles Lorgeril.

Monastrell – Black grape variety of Spain, widely planted in Mediterranean regions for inexpensive wines notable for their high alcohol and toughness – though they can mature into excellent, soft reds. The variety is known in France as Mourvèdre and in Australia as Mataro.

Monbazillac – AC for sweet, dessert wines within the wider appellation of Bergerac in south-west France. Made from the same grape varieties (principally Sauvignon and Semillon) that go into the much costlier counterpart wines of Barsac and Sauternes near Bordeaux, these stickies from botrytis-affected, late-harvested grapes can be delicious and good value for money.

Montalcino – Hill town of Tuscany, Italy, and a DOCG for strong and very long-lived red wines from Brunello grapes. The wines are mostly very expensive. Rosso di Montalcino, a DOC for the humbler wines of the zone, is often a good buy.

Montepulciano – Black grape variety of Italy. Best known in Montepulciano d'Abruzzo, the juicy, purply-black and bramble-fruited red of the Abruzzi region midway down Italy's Adriatic side. Also the grape in the rightly popular hearty reds of Rosso Conero from around Ancona in the Marches. Not to be confused with the hill town of Montepulciano in Tuscany, famous for expensive Vino Nobile di Montepulciano wine.

morello – Lots of red wines have smells and flavours redolent of cherries. Morello cherries, among the darkest coloured and sweetest of all varieties and the preferred choice of cherry-brandy producers, have a distinct sweetness resembled by some wines made from Merlot grapes. A morello whiff or taste is generally very welcome.

Moscatel – Spanish Muscat.

Moscato – *See* Muscat.

Moselle – The wine of Germany's Mosel river valleys, collectively known for winemaking purposes as Mosel-Saar-Ruwer. The wine always comes in slim, green bottles, as distinct from the brown bottles traditionally, but no longer exclusively, employed for Rhine wines.

Mourvèdre – Widely planted black grape variety of southern France. It's an ingredient in many of the wines of Provence, the Rhône and Languedoc, including the ubiquitous Vin de Pays d'Oc. It's a hot-climate vine and the wine is usually blended with other varieties to give sweet aromas and 'backbone' to the mix. Known as Mataro in Australia and Monastrell in Spain.

Muscadet – One of France's most familiar everyday whites, made from a grape called the Melon or Melon de Bourgogne. It comes from vineyards at the estuarial end of the River Loire, and has a sea-breezy freshness about it. The better wines are reckoned to be those from the vineyards in the Sèvre et Maine region, and many are made *sur lie* – 'on the lees' – meaning that the wine is left in contact with the yeasty deposit of its fermentation until just before bottling, in an endeavour to add interest to what can sometimes be an acidic and fruitless style.

Muscat – Grape variety with origins in ancient Greece, and still grown widely among the Aegean islands for the production of sweet white wines. Muscats are the wines that taste more like grape juice than any other – but the high sugar levels ensure they are also among the most alcoholic of wines, too. Known as Moscato in Italy, the grape is much used for making sweet sparkling wines, as in Asti Spumante or Moscato d'Asti. There are several appellations in south-west France for inexpensive Muscats made rather like port, part-fermented before the addition of grape alcohol to halt the conversion of sugar into alcohol, creating a sweet and heady *vin doux naturel*. Dry Muscat wines, when well made, have a delicious sweet aroma but a refreshing, light touch with flavours reminiscent variously of orange blossom, wood smoke and grapefruit.

must – New-pressed grape juice prior to fermentation.

N

Navarra – DO wine-producing region of northern Spain adjacent to, and overshadowed by, Rioja. Navarra's wines can be startlingly akin to their neighbouring rivals, and sometimes rather better value for money.

négociant – In France, a dealer-producer who buys wines from growers and matures and/or blends them for sale under his or her own label. Purists can be a bit sniffy about these entrepreneurs, claiming that only the vine-grower with his or her own winemaking set-up can make truly authentic stuff, but the truth is that many of the best wines of France are *négociant*-produced – especially at the humbler end of the price scale. *Négociants* are often identified on wine labels as *négociant-éleveur* (literally 'dealer-bringer-up'), meaning that the wine has been matured, blended and bottled by the party in question.

Negroamaro – Black grape variety mainly of Puglia, the much-lauded wine region of south-east Italy. Dense, earthy red wines with ageing potential and plenty of alcohol. The grape behind Copertino, Salice Salentio and Squinzano.

Nerello Mascalese – Black grape of Sicily making light, flavoursome and alcoholic reds.

Nero d'Avola – Black grape variety of Sicily and southern Italy. It makes deep-coloured wines that, given half a chance, can develop intensity and richness with age.

non-vintage – A wine is described as such when it has been blended from the harvests of more than one year. A non-vintage wine is not necessarily an inferior one, but under quality-control regulations around the world, still table wines most usually derive solely from one year's grape crop to qualify for appellation status. Champagnes and sparkling wines are mostly blended from several vintages, as are fortified wines, such as basic port and sherry.

nose – In the vocabulary of the wine-taster, the nose is the scent of a wine. Sounds a bit dotty, but it makes a sensible enough alternative to the rather bald 'smell'. The use of the word 'perfume' implies that the wine smells particularly good. 'Aroma' is used specifically to describe a wine that smells as it should, as in 'this burgundy has the authentic strawberry-raspberry aroma of Pinot Noir'.

O

oak – Most of the world's costliest wines are matured in new or nearly new oak barrels, giving additional opulence of flavour. Of late, many cheaper wines have been getting the oak treatment, too, in older, cheaper casks, or simply by having sacks of oak chippings poured into their steel or fibreglass holding tanks. 'Oak aged' on a label is likely to indicate the latter treatments. But the overtly oaked wines of Australia have in some cases been so overdone that there is now a reactive trend whereby some producers proclaim their wines – particularly Chardonnays – as 'unoaked' on the label, thereby asserting that the flavours are more naturally achieved.

Oltrepo Pavese – Wine-producing zone of Piedmont, north-west Italy. The name means 'south of Pavia across the [river] Po' and the wines, both white and red, can be excellent quality and value for money.

organic wine – As in other sectors of the food industry, demand for organically made wine is – or appears to be – growing. As a rule, a wine qualifies as organic if it comes entirely from grapes grown in vineyards cultivated without the use of synthetic materials, and made in a winery where chemical treatments or additives are shunned with similar vigour. In fact, there are plenty of winemakers in the world using organic methods, but who disdain to label their bottles as such. Wines proclaiming their organic status used to carry the same sort of premium as their counterparts round the corner in the fruit, vegetable and meat aisles. But organic viticulture is now commonplace and there seems little price impact. There is no single worldwide (or even Europe-wide) standard for organic food or wine, so you pretty much have to take the producer's word for it.

P

Pasqua – One of the biggest and, it should be said, best wine producers of the Veneto region of north-west Italy.

Passetoutgrains – Bourgogne Passetoutgrains is a generic appellation of the Burgundy region, France. The word loosely means 'any grapes allowed' and is supposed specifically to designate a red wine made with Gamay grapes as well as Burgundy's principal black variety, Pinot Noir, in a ratio of two parts Gamay to one of Pinot. The wine is usually relatively inexpensive, and relatively uninteresting, too.

Pays d'Oc – Shortened form under recent rule changes of French wine designation Vin de Pays d'Oc. All other similar regional designations can be similarly abbreviated.

Pecorino – White grape variety of mid-eastern Italy currently in vogue for well-coloured dry white varietal wines.

Periquita – Black grape variety of southern Portugal. Makes rather exotic spicy reds. Name means 'parrot'.

Perricone – Black grape variety of Sicily. Low-acid red wines.

PET – It's what they call plastic wine bottles – lighter to transport and allegedly as ecological as glass. Polyethylene terephthalate.

Petit Verdot – Black grape variety of Bordeaux used to give additional colour, density and spiciness to Cabernet Sauvignon-dominated blends. Mostly a minority player at home, but in Australia and California it is grown as the principal variety for some big hearty reds of real character.

petrol – When white wines from certain grapes, especially Riesling, are allowed to age in the bottle for longer than a year or two, they can take on a spirity aroma reminiscent of petrol or diesel. In grand mature German wines, this is considered a very good thing.

Picpoul – Grape variety of southern France. Best known in Picpoul de Pinet, a dry white from near Carcassonne in the Languedoc, newly elevated to AOP status. The name Picpoul (also Piquepoul) means 'stings the lips' – referring to the natural high acidity of the juice.

Piemonte – North-western province of Italy, which we call Piedmont, known for the spumante wines of the town of Asti, plus expensive Barbaresco and Barolo and better-value varietal red wines from Barbera and Dolcetto grapes.

Pinotage – South Africa's own black grape variety. Makes red wines ranging from light and juicy to dark, strong and long-lived. It's a cross between Pinot Noir and a grape the South Africans used to call Hermitage (thus the portmanteau name) but turns out to have been Cinsault.

Pinot Blanc – White grape variety principally of Alsace, France. Florally perfumed, exotically fruity dry white wines.

Pinot Grigio – White grape variety of northern Italy. Wines bearing its name are perplexingly fashionable. Good examples have an interesting smoky-pungent aroma and keen, slaking fruit. But most are dull. Originally French, it is at its best in the lushly exotic Pinot Gris wines of Alsace and is also successfully cultivated in Germany and New Zealand.

Pinot Noir – The great black grape of Burgundy, France. It makes all the region's fabulously expensive red wines. Notoriously difficult to grow in warmer climates, it is nevertheless cultivated by countless intrepid winemakers in the New World intent on reproducing the magic appeal of red burgundy. California and New Zealand have come closest, but rarely at prices much below those for the real thing. Some Chilean Pinot Noirs are inexpensive and worth trying.

Pouilly Fuissé – Village and AC of the Mâconnais region of southern Burgundy in France. Dry white wines from Chardonnay grapes. Wines are among the highest rated of the Mâconnais.

Pouilly Fumé – Village and AC of the Loire Valley in France. Dry white wines from Sauvignon Blanc grapes. Similar 'pebbly', 'grassy' or even 'gooseberry' style to neighbouring AC Sancerre. The notion put about by some enthusiasts that Pouilly Fumé is 'smoky' is surely nothing more than word association with the name.

Primitivo – Black grape variety of southern Italy, especially the region of Puglia. Named from Latin *primus* for first, the grape is among the earliest-ripening of all varieties. The wines are typically dense and dark in colour with plenty of alcohol, and have an earthy, spicy style. Often a real bargain.

Priorat – Emerging wine region of Catalonia, Spain. Highly valued red wines from Garnacha and other varieties.

Prosecco – White grape variety of Italy's Veneto region known entirely for the softly sparkling wine it makes. The best come from the DOCG Conegliano-Valdobbiadene, made as spumante ('foaming') wines in pressurised tanks, typically to 11 per cent alcohol and ranging from softly sweet to crisply dry. Now trendy, but the cheap wines – one leading brand comes in a can – are of very variable quality.

Puglia – The region occupying the 'heel' of southern Italy, lately making many good, inexpensive wines from indigenous grape varieties.

Q

QbA – German, standing for Qualitätswein bestimmter Anbaugebiete. It means 'quality wine from designated areas' and implies that the wine is made from grapes with a minimum level of ripeness, but it's by no means a guarantee of exciting quality. Only wines labelled QmP (see next entry) can be depended upon to be special.

QmP – Stands for Qualitätswein mit Prädikat. These are the serious wines of Germany, made without the addition of sugar to 'improve' them. To qualify for QmP status, the grapes must reach a level of ripeness as measured on a sweetness scale – all according to Germany's fiendishly complicated wine-quality regulations. Wines from grapes that reach the stated minimum level of sweetness qualify for the description of Kabinett. The next level up earns the rank of Spätlese, meaning 'late-picked'. Kabinett wines can be expected to be dry and brisk in style, and Spätlese wines a little bit riper and fuller. The next grade up, Auslese, meaning 'selected harvest', indicates a wine made from super-ripe grapes; it will be golden in colour and honeyed in flavour. A generation ago, these wines were as valued, and as expensive, as any of the world's grandest appellations.

Quincy – AC of Loire Valley, France, known for pebbly-dry white wines from Sauvignon grapes. The wines are forever compared to those of nearby and much better-known Sancerre – and Quincy often represents better value for money. Pronounced 'KAN-see'.

Quinta – Portuguese for farm or estate. It precedes the names of many of Portugal's best-known wines. It is pronounced 'KEEN-ta'.

R

racy – Evocative wine-tasting description for wine that thrills the tastebuds with a rush of exciting sensations. Good Rieslings often qualify.

raisiny – Wines from grapes that have been very ripe or overripe at harvest can take on a smell and flavour akin to the concentrated, heat-dried sweetness of raisins. As a minor element in the character of a wine, this can add to the appeal but as a dominant characteristic it is a fault.

rancio – Spanish term harking back to Roman times when wines were commonly stored in jars outside, exposed to the sun, so they oxidised and took on a burnt sort of flavour. Today, *rancio* describes a baked – and by no means unpleasant – flavour in fortified wines, particularly sherry and Madeira.

Reserva – In Portugal and Spain, this has genuine significance. The Portuguese use it for special wines with a higher alcohol level and longer ageing, although the precise periods vary between regions. In Spain, especially in the Navarra and Rioja regions, it means the wine must have had at least a year in oak and two in bottle before release.

reserve – On French (as *réserve*) or other wines, this implies special-quality, longer-aged wines, but has no official significance.

Retsina – The universal white wine of Greece. It has been traditionally made in Attica, the region of Athens, for a very long time, and is said to owe its origins and name to the ancient custom of sealing amphorae (terracotta jars) of the wine with a gum made from pine resin. Some of the flavour of the resin inevitably transmitted itself into the wine, and ancient Greeks acquired a lasting taste for it.

Reuilly – AC of Loire Valley, France, for crisp dry whites from Sauvignon grapes. Pronounced 'RER-yee'.

Ribatejo – Emerging wine region of Portugal. Worth seeking out on labels of red wines in particular, because new winemakers are producing lively stuff from distinctive indigenous grapes such as Castelao and Trincadeira.

Ribera del Duero – Classic wine region of north-west Spain lying along the River Duero (which crosses the border to become Portugal's Douro, forming the valley where port comes from). It is home to an estate rather oddly named Vega Sicilia, where red wines of epic quality are made and sold at equally epic prices. Further down the scale, some very good reds are made, too.

Riesling – The noble grape variety of Germany. It is correctly pronounced 'REEZ-ling', not 'RICE-ling'. Once notorious as the grape behind all those boring 'medium' Liebfraumilches and Niersteiners, this grape has had a bad press. In fact, there has never been much, if any, Riesling in Germany's cheap-and-nasty plonks. But the country's best wines, the so-called Qualitätswein mit Prädikat grades, are made almost exclusively with Riesling. These wines range from crisply fresh and appley styles to extravagantly fruity, honeyed wines from late-harvested grapes. Excellent Riesling wines are also made in Alsace and now in Australia.

Rioja – The principal fine-wine region of Spain, in the country's north east. The pricier wines are noted for their vanilla-pod richness from long ageing in oak casks. Tempranillo and Garnacha grapes make the reds, Viura the whites.

Ripasso – A particular style of Valpolicella wine. New wine is partially refermented in vats that have been used to make the Recioto reds (wines made from semi-dried grapes), thus creating a bigger, smoother version of usually light and pale Valpolicella.

Riserva – In Italy, a wine made only in the best vintages, and allowed longer ageing in cask and bottle.

Rivaner – Alternative name for Germany's Müller-Thurgau grape, the life-blood of Liebfraumilch.

Riverland – Vineyard region to the immediate north of the Barossa Valley of South Australia, extending east into New South Wales.

Roditis – White grape variety of Greece, known for fresh dry whites with decent acidity, often included in retsina.

rosso – Red wine, Italy.

Rosso Conero – DOC red wine made in the environs of Ancona in the Marches, Italy. Made from the Montepulciano grape, the wine can provide excellent value for money.

Ruby Cabernet – Black grape variety of California, created by crossing Cabernet Sauvignon and Carignan. Makes soft and squelchy red wine at home and in South Africa.

Rueda – DO of north-west Spain making first-class refreshing dry whites from the indigenous Verdejo grape, imported Sauvignon, and others. Exciting quality, and prices are keen.

Rully – AC of Chalonnais region of southern Burgundy, France. White wines from Chardonnay and red wines from Pinot Noir grapes. Both can be very good and are substantially cheaper than their more northerly Burgundian neighbours. Pronounced 'ROO-yee'.

S

Saint Emilion – AC of Bordeaux, France. Centred on the romantic hill town of St Emilion, this famous sub-region makes some of the grandest red wines of France, but also some of the best-value ones. Less fashionable than the Médoc region on the opposite (west) bank of the River Gironde that bisects Bordeaux, St Emilion wines are made largely with the Merlot grape, and are relatively quick to mature. The top wines are classified *1er grand cru classé* and are madly expensive, but many more are classified respectively *grand cru classé* and *grand cru*, and these designations can be seen as a fairly trustworthy indicator of quality. There are several 'satellite' St Emilion ACs named after the villages at their centres, notably Lussac St Emilion, Montagne St Emilion and Puisseguin St Emilion. Some excellent wines are made by estates within these ACs, and at relatively affordable prices thanks to the comparatively humble status of their satellite designations.

Salento – Up-and-coming wine region of southern Italy. Many good bargain reds from local grapes including Nero d'Avola and Primitivo.

Sancerre – AC of the Loire Valley, France, renowned for flinty-fresh Sauvignon whites and rarer Pinot Noir reds. These wines are never cheap, and recent tastings make it plain that only the best-made, individual-producer wines are worth the money. Budget brands seem mostly dull.

Sangiovese – The local black grape of Tuscany, Italy. It is the principal variety used for Chianti and is now widely planted in Latin America – often making delicious, Chianti-like wines with characteristic cherryish-but-deeply-ripe fruit and a dry, clean finish. Chianti wines have become (unjustifiably) expensive in recent years and cheaper Italian wines such as those called Sangiovese di Toscana make a consoling substitute.

Saumur – Town and appellation of Loire Valley, France. Characterful minerally red wines from Cabernet Franc grapes, and some whites. The once-popular sparkling wines from Chenin Blanc grapes are now little seen in Britain.

Saumur-Champigny – Separate appellation for red wines from Cabernet Franc grapes of Saumur in the Loire, sometimes very good and lively.

Sauvignon Blanc – French white grape variety now grown worldwide. New Zealand is successfully challenging the long supremacy of French ACs such as Sancerre. The wines are characterised by aromas of gooseberry, fresh-cut grass, even asparagus. Flavours are often described as 'grassy' or 'nettly'.

sec – Dry wine style. French.

secco – Dry wine style. Italian.

Semillon – White grape variety originally of Bordeaux, where it is blended with Sauvignon Blanc to make fresh dry whites and, when harvested very late in the season, the ambrosial sweet whites of Barsac, Sauternes and other appellations. Even in the driest wines, the grape can be recognised from its honeyed, sweet-pineapple, even banana-like aromas. Now widely planted in Australia and Latin America, and frequently blended with Chardonnay to make dry whites, some of them interesting.

sherry – The great aperitif wine of Spain, centred on the Andalusian city of Jerez (from which the name 'sherry' is an English mispronunciation). There is a lot of sherry-style wine in the world, but only the authentic wine from Jerez and the neighbouring producing towns of Puerta de Santa Maria and Sanlucar de Barrameda may label their wines as such. The Spanish drink real sherry – very dry and fresh, pale in colour and served well-chilled – called fino and manzanilla, and darker but naturally dry variations called amontillado, palo cortado and oloroso.

Shiraz – Australian name for the Syrah grape. The variety is the most widely planted of any in Australia, and makes red wines of wildly varying quality, characterised by dense colour, high alcohol, spicy fruit and generous, cushiony texture.

Somontano – Wine region of north-east Spain. Name means 'under the mountains' – in this case the Pyrenees – and the region has had DO status since 1984. Much innovative winemaking here, with New World styles emerging. Some very good buys. A region to watch.

souple – French wine-tasting term that translates into English as 'supple' or even 'docile' as in 'pliable', but I understand it in the vinous context to mean muscular but soft – a wine with tannin as well as soft fruit.

Spätlese – *See* QmP.

spirity – Some wines, mostly from the New World, are made from grapes so ripe at harvest that their high alcohol content can be detected through a mildly burning sensation on the tongue, similar to the effect of sipping a spirit.

spritzy – Describes a wine with a barely detectable sparkle. Some young wines are intended to have this elusive fizziness; in others it is a fault.

spumante – Sparkling wine of Italy. Asti Spumante is the best known, from the town of Asti in the north-west Italian province of Piemonte.

The term describes wines that are fully sparkling. Frizzante wines have a less vigorous mousse.

stalky – A useful tasting term to describe red wines with flavours that make you think the stalks from the grape bunches must have been fermented along with the must (juice). Young Bordeaux reds very often have this mild astringency. In moderation it's fine, but if it dominates it probably signifies the wine is at best immature and at worst badly made.

Stellenbosch – Town and region at the heart of South Africa's burgeoning wine industry. It's an hour's drive from Cape Town and the source of much of the country's cheaper wine. Quality is variable, and the name Stellenbosch on a label can't (yet, anyway) be taken as a guarantee of quality.

stony – Wine-tasting term for keenly dry white wines. It's meant to indicate a wine of purity and real quality, with just the right match of fruit and acidity.

structured – Good wines are not one-dimensional, they have layers of flavour and texture. A structured wine has phases of enjoyment: the 'attack', or first impression in the mouth; the middle palate as the wine is held in the mouth; and the lingering aftertaste.

summer fruit – Wine-tasting term intended to convey a smell or taste of soft fruits such as strawberries and raspberries – without having to commit too specifically to which.

superiore – On labels of Italian wines, this is more than an idle boast. Under DOC rules, wines must qualify for the *superiore* designation by reaching one or more specified quality levels, usually a higher alcohol content or an additional period of maturation. Frascati, for example, qualifies for DOC status at 11.5 per cent alcohol, but to be classified *superiore* must have 12 per cent alcohol.

sur lie – Literally, 'on the lees'. It's a term now widely used on the labels of Muscadet wines, signifying that after fermentation has died down, the new wine has been left in the tank over the winter on the lees – the detritus of yeasts and other interesting compounds left over from the turbid fermentation process. The idea is that additional interest is imparted into the flavour of the wine.

Syrah – The noble grape of the Rhône Valley, France. Makes very dark, dense wine characterised by peppery, tarry aromas. Now planted all over southern France and farther afield. In Australia, where it makes wines ranging from disagreeably jam-like plonks to wonderfully rich and silky keeping wines, it is known as Shiraz.

T

table wine – Wine that is unfortified and of an alcoholic strength, for UK tax purposes anyway, of no more than 15 per cent. I use the term to distinguish, for example, between the red table wines of the Douro Valley in Portugal and the region's better-known fortified wine, port.

Tafelwein – Table wine, German. The humblest quality designation, which doesn't usually bode very well.

tank method – Bulk-production process for sparkling wines. Base wine undergoes secondary fermentation in a large, sealed vat rather than in individual closed bottles. Also known as the Charmat method after the name of the inventor of the process.

Tai – White grape variety of north-east Italy, a relative of Sauvignon Blanc. Also known in Italy as Tocai Friulano or, more correctly, Friulano.

Tannat – Black grape of south-west France, notably for wines of Madiran, and lately named as the variety most beneficial to health thanks to its outstanding antioxidant content.

tannin – Well known as the film-forming, teeth-coating component in tea, tannin is a natural compound that occurs in black grape skins and acts as a natural preservative in wine. Its noticeable presence in wine is regarded as a good thing. It gives young everyday reds their dryness, firmness of flavour and backbone. And it helps high-quality reds to retain their lively fruitiness for many years. A grand Bordeaux red when first made, for example, will have purply-sweet, rich fruit and mouth-puckering tannin, but after ten years or so this will have evolved into a delectably fruity, mature wine in which the formerly parching effects of the tannin have receded almost completely, leaving the shade of 'residual tannin' that marks out a great wine approaching maturity.

Tarrango – Black grape variety of Australia.

tarry – On the whole, winemakers don't like critics to say their wines evoke the redolence of road repairs, but I can't help using this term to describe the agreeable, sweet, 'burnt' flavour that is often found at the centre of the fruit in wines from Argentina, Italy and Portugal in particular.

TCA – Dreaded ailment in wine, usually blamed on faulty corks. It stands for 246 *trichloroanisol* and is characterised by a horrible musty smell and flavour in the affected wine. It is largely because of the current plague of TCA that so many wine producers worldwide are now going over to polymer 'corks' and screwcaps.

tears – The colourless alcohol in the wine left clinging to the inside of the glass after the contents have been swirled. Persistent tears (also known as 'legs') indicate a wine of good concentration.

Tempranillo – The great black grape of Spain. Along with Garnacha (Grenache in France) it makes all red Rioja and Navarra wines and, under many pseudonyms, is an important or exclusive contributor to the wines of many other regions of Spain. It is also widely cultivated in South America.

Teroldego – Black grape variety of Trentino, northern Italy. Often known as Teroldego Rotaliano after the Rotaliano region where most of the vineyards lie. Deep-coloured, assertive, green-edged red wines.

tinto – On Spanish labels indicates a deeply coloured red wine. Clarete denotes a paler colour. Also Portuguese.

Toro – Quality wine region east of Zamora, Spain.

Torrontes – White grape variety of Argentina. Makes soft, dry wines often with delicious grapey-spicy aroma, similar in style to the classic dry Muscat wines of Alsace, but at more accessible prices.

Touraine – Region encompassing a swathe of the Loire Valley, France. Non-AC wines may be labelled 'Sauvignon de Touraine' etc.

Touriga Nacional – The most valued black grape variety of the Douro Valley in Portugal, where port is made. The name Touriga now appears on an increasing number of table wines made as sidelines by the port producers. They can be very good, with the same spirity aroma and sleek flavours of port itself, minus the fortification.

Traminer – Grape variety, the same as Gewürztraminer.

Trebbiano – The workhorse white grape of Italy. A productive variety that is easy to cultivate, it seems to be included in just about every ordinary white wine of the entire nation – including Frascati, Orvieto and Soave. It is the same grape as France's Ugni Blanc. There are, however, distinct regional variations of the grape. Trebbiano di Lugana makes a distinctive white in the DOC of the name, sometimes very good, while Trebbiano di Toscana makes a major contribution to the distinctly less interesting dry whites of Chianti country.

Trincadeira Preta – Portuguese black grape variety native to the port-producing vineyards of the Douro Valley (where it goes under the name Tinta Amarella). In southern Portugal, it produces dark and sturdy table wines.

trocken – 'Dry' German wine. It's a recent trend among commercial-scale producers in the Rhine and Mosel to label their wines with this description in the hope of reassuring consumers that the contents do not resemble the dreaded sugar-water Liebfraumilch-type plonks of the bad old days. But the description does have a particular meaning under German wine law, namely that there is only a low level of unfermented sugar lingering in the wine (9 grams per litre, if you need to know), and this can leave the wine tasting rather austere.

U

Ugni Blanc – The most widely cultivated white grape variety of France and the mainstay of many a cheap dry white wine. To date it has been better known as the provider of base wine for distilling into armagnac and cognac, but lately the name has been appearing on wine labels. Technology seems to be improving the performance of the grape. The curious name is pronounced 'OON-yee', and is the same variety as Italy's ubiquitous Trebbiano.

Utiel-Requena – Region and *Denominación de Origen* of Mediterranean Spain inland from Valencia. Principally red wines from Bobal, Garnacha and Tempranillo grapes grown at relatively high altitude, between 600 and 900 metres.

V

Vacqueyras – Village of the southern Rhône Valley of France in the region better known for its generic appellation, the Côtes du Rhône. Vacqueyras can date its winemaking history all the way back to 1414, but has only been producing under its own village AC since 1991. The wines, from Grenache and Syrah grapes, can be wonderfully silky and intense, spicy and long-lived.

Valdepeñas – An island of quality production amidst the ocean of mediocrity that is Spain's La Mancha region – where most of the grapes are grown for distilling into the head-banging brandies of Jerez. Valdepeñas reds are made from a grape they call the Cencibel – which turns out to be a very close relation of the Tempranillo grape that is the mainstay of the fine but expensive red wines of Rioja. Again, like Rioja, Valdepeñas wines are matured in oak casks to give them a vanilla-rich smoothness. Among bargain reds, Valdepeñas is a name to look out for.

Valpolicella – Red wine of Verona, Italy. Good examples have ripe, cherry fruit and a pleasingly dry finish. Unfortunately, there are many bad examples of Valpolicella. Shop with circumspection. Valpolicella Classico wines, from the best vineyards clustered around the town, are more reliable. Those additionally labelled *superiore* have higher alcohol and some bottle age.

vanilla – Ageing wines in oak barrels (or, less picturesquely, adding oak chips to wine in huge concrete vats) imparts a range of characteristics including a smell of vanilla from the ethyl vanilline naturally given off by oak.

varietal – A varietal wine is one named after the grape variety (one or more) from which it is made. Nearly all everyday wines worldwide are now labelled in this way. It is salutary to contemplate that until the present wine boom began in the 1980s, wines described thus were virtually unknown outside Germany and one or two quirky regions of France and Italy.

vegan-friendly – My informal way of noting that a wine is claimed to have been made not only with animal-product-free finings (*see* vegetarian wine) but without any animal-related products whatsoever, such as manure in the vineyards.

vegetal – A tasting note definitely open to interpretation. It suggests a smell or flavour reminiscent less of fruit (apple, pineapple, strawberry and the like) than of something leafy or even root based. Some wines are evocative (to some tastes) of beetroot, cabbage or even unlikelier vegetable flavours – and these characteristics may add materially to the attraction of the wine.

vegetarian wine – Wines labelled 'suitable for vegetarians' have been made without the assistance of animal products for 'fining' – clarifying – before bottling. Gelatine, egg whites, isinglass from fish bladders and casein from milk are among the items shunned, usually in favour of bentonite, an absorbent clay first found at Benton in the US state of Montana.

Verdejo – White grape of the Rueda region in north-west Spain. It can make superbly perfumed crisp dry whites of truly distinctive character and has helped make Rueda one of the best white-wine sources of Europe. No relation to Verdelho.

Verdelho – Portuguese grape variety once mainly used for a medium-dry style of Madeira, also called Verdelho, but now rare. The vine is now prospering in Australia, where it can make well-balanced dry whites with fleeting richness and lemon-lime acidity.

Verdicchio – White grape variety of Italy best known in the DOC zone of Castelli di Jesi in the Adriatic wine region of the Marches. Dry white wines once known for little more than their naff amphora-style bottles but now gaining a reputation for interesting, herbaceous flavours of recognisable character.

Vermentino – White grape variety principally of Italy, especially Sardinia. Makes florally scented soft dry whites.

Vieilles vignes – Old vines. Many French producers like to claim on their labels that the wine within is from vines of notable antiquity. While it's true that vines don't produce useful grapes for the first few years after planting, it is uncertain whether vines of much greater age – say 25 years plus – than others actually make better fruit. There are no regulations governing the use of the term, so it's not a reliable indicator anyway.

Vin de France – In effect, the new Vin de Table of France's morphing wine laws. The term Vin de Table has just about disappeared – or should have, under new legislation introduced in 2010 – and Vin de France installed as the designation of a wine guaranteed to have been produced in France. The label may state the vintage (if all the wine in the blend does come from a single year's harvest) and the grape varieties that constitute the wine. It may not state the region of France from which the wine comes.

vin de liqueur – Sweet style of white wine mostly from the Pyrenean region of south-westernmost France, made by adding a little spirit to the new wine before it has fermented out, halting the fermentation and retaining sugar.

vin de pays – 'Country wine' of France. The French map is divided up into more than 100 vin de pays regions. Wine in bottles labelled as such must be from grapes grown in the nominated zone or *département*. Some vin de pays areas are huge: the Vin de Pays d'Oc (named after the Languedoc region) covers much of the Midi and Provence. Plenty of wines bearing this humble designation are of astoundingly high quality and certainly compete with New World counterparts for interest and value. *See* Indication Géographique Protégée.

vin de table – The humblest official classification of French wine. Neither the region, grape varieties nor vintage need be stated on the label. The wine might not even be French. Don't expect too much from this kind of 'table wine'. *See* Vin de France.

vin doux naturel – Sweet, mildly fortified wine of southern France. A little spirit is added during the winemaking process, halting the fermentation by killing the yeast before it has consumed all the sugars – hence the pronounced sweetness of the wine.

vin gris – Rosé wine from Provence.

Vinho de mesa – 'Table wine' of Portugal.

Vino da tavola – The humblest official classification of Italian wine. Much ordinary plonk bears this designation, but the bizarre quirks of Italy's wine laws dictate that some of that country's finest wines are also classed as mere vino da tavola (table wine). If an expensive Italian wine is labelled as such, it doesn't mean it will be a disappointment.

Vino de mesa – 'Table wine' of Spain. Usually very ordinary.

vintage – The grape harvest. The year displayed on bottle labels is the year of the harvest. Wines bearing no date have been blended from the harvests of two or more years.

Viognier – A grape variety once exclusive to the northern Rhône Valley in France where it makes a very chi-chi wine, Condrieu, usually costing £20 plus. Now, the Viognier is grown more widely, in North and South America as well as elsewhere in France, and occasionally produces soft, marrowy whites that echo the grand style of Condrieu itself. The Viognier is now commonly blended with Shiraz in red winemaking in Australia and South Africa. It does not dilute the colour and is confidently believed by highly experienced winemakers to enhance the quality. Steve Webber, in charge of winemaking at the revered De Bortoli estates in the Yarra Valley region of Victoria, Australia, puts between two and five per cent Viognier in with some of his Shiraz wines. 'I think it's the perfume,' he told me. 'It gives some femininity to the wine.'

Viura – White grape variety of Rioja, Spain. Also widely grown elsewhere in Spain under the name Macabeo. Wines have a blossomy aroma and are dry, but sometimes soft at the expense of acidity.

Vouvray – AC of the Loire Valley, France, known for still and sparkling dry white wines and sweet, still whites from late-harvested grapes. The wines, all from Chenin Blanc grapes, have a unique capacity for unctuous softness combined with lively freshness – an effect best portrayed in the demi-sec (slightly sweet) wines, which can be delicious and keenly priced. Unfashionable, but worth looking out for.

Vranac – Black grape variety of the Balkans known for dense colour and tangy-bitter edge to the flavour. Best enjoyed in situ.

W

weight – In an ideal world the weight of a wine is determined by the ripeness of the grapes from which it has been made. In some cases the weight is determined merely by the quantity of sugar added during the production process. A good, genuine wine described as having weight is one in which there is plenty of alcohol and 'extract' – colour and flavour from the grapes. Wine enthusiasts judge weight by swirling the wine in the glass and then examining the 'legs' or 'tears' left clinging to the inside of the glass after the contents have subsided. Alcohol gives these runlets a dense, glycerine-like condition, and if they cling for a long time, the wine is deemed to have weight – a very good thing in all honestly made wines.

Winzergenossenschaft – One of the many very lengthy and peculiar words regularly found on labels of German wines. This means a winemaking co-operative. Many excellent German wines are made by these associations of growers.

woodsap – A subjective tasting note. Some wines have a fleeting bitterness, which is not a fault, but an interesting balancing factor amidst very ripe flavours. The effect somehow evokes woodsap.

X

Xarel-lo – One of the main grape varieties for cava, the sparkling wine of Spain.

Xinomavro – Black grape variety of Greece. It retains its acidity even in the very hot conditions that prevail in many Greek vineyards, where harvests tend to over-ripen and make cooked-tasting wines. Modern winemaking techniques are capable of making well-balanced wines from Xinomavro.

Y

Yecla – Town and DO wine region of eastern Spain, close to Alicante, making lots of interesting, strong-flavoured red and white wines, often at bargain prices.

yellow – White wines are not white at all, but various shades of yellow – or, more poetically, gold. Some white wines with opulent richness even have a flavour I cannot resist calling yellow – reminiscent of butter.

Z

Zibibbo – Sicilian white grape variety synonymous with north African variety Muscat of Alexandria. Scantily employed in sweet winemaking, and occasionally for drier styles.

Zinfandel – Black grape variety of California. Makes brambly reds, some of which can age very gracefully, and 'blush' whites – actually pink, because a little of the skin colour is allowed to leach into the must. The vine is also planted in Australia and South America. The Primitivo of southern Italy is said to be a related variety, but makes a very different kind of wine.

Index